U1003271

非物质文化遗产档案

中华老字号·宜兴金鱼紫砂陶瓷酒瓶烧造技艺

系国家社会科学基金艺术学课题项目系列成果之一

批准号：11CG125

The Intangible Cultural Heritage File

China Time-honored Brand · Yixing Baking Crafts of Yixing Goldfish Purple Ceramic Wine Bottle

Project of Arts Science of the National Social Science Foundation

Project Grant No. 11CG125

文化部科技司
全国艺术科学规划领导小组办公室
Department of Science and Technology of Ministry of Culture
National leading group office of art-related science and technology

宜兴金鱼紫砂陶瓷酒瓶烧造技艺

老字号文化遗产保护工程重点研究项目

编号：20101019

Yixing Baking Crafts of Yixing Goldfish Purple Ceramic Wine Bottle

Key Research Project on Time-honored Brand Cultural Heritage Protection

Serial No. 20100019

藝術團隊孙冬宁作品
Production of Sun Dongning in ART TEAMWORK
yishutuandui@yahoo.com.cn

非物质文化遗产档案

中华老字号·宜兴金鱼紫砂陶瓷酒瓶烧造技艺

China Time-honored Brand·Yixing Baking Crafts of Yixing Goldfish Purple Ceramic Wine Bottle

孙冬宁／著
Composer Sun Dongning

文化艺術出版社
Culture and Art Publishing House

非物质文化遗产档案

申报国家级非物质文化遗产名录图像文本

Image and Text of Declaration for National Intangible Cultual Heritage List

文化艺术出版社

Culture and Art Publishing House

宜兴金鱼紫砂陶瓷酒瓶

Yixing Goldfish Purple Ceramic Wine Bottle

烧造技艺

B a k i n g　C r a f t s

孙冬宁／著

Composer Sun Dongning

文化艺术出版社

Culture and Art Publishing House

非物质文化遗产档案

宜兴金鱼紫砂陶瓷酒瓶烧造技艺·老字号文化遗产保护工程重点研究项目

课题立项号：20100019

项目组负责人

谈志坚

研究组负责人

孙冬宁

课题组成员

谈　珂　刘　兴　鲍玉麟　高　辉　朱慧慧　潘云光　周顺元

石军良　吕　焰　李义勇　何　梁　杨　凡　朱宏轩

田野调查

山东非物质文化遗产研究中心田野考察队

口述实录调查小组成员

何　梁　杨　凡　赵春海　杨　飞　王安琪　李　成

The Intangible Cultural Heritage File

Yixing Baking Crafts of Yixing Goldfish Purple Ceramic Wine Bottle

Key Research Project on Time-honored Brand Cultural Heritage Protection

Project No. 20100019

Person in Charge of the Project Team

Tan Zhijian

Person in Charge of the Research Group

Sun Dongning

Members of the Research Group

Tan Ke, Liu Xing, Bao Yulin, Gao Hui, Zhu Huihui, Pan Yunguang, Zhou Shunyuan

Shi Junliang, Lv Yan, Li Yiyong, He Liang, Yang Fan, Zhu Hongxuan

Field Investigation

Field Investigation Team of Research Center of the Intangible Cultural Heritage in Shandong

Survey Members of Oral Record

He Liang, Yang Fan, Zhao Chunhai, Yang Fei, Wang Anqi, Li Cheng

非物质文化遗产档案

中华老字号·宜兴金鱼紫砂陶瓷酒瓶烧造技艺

特邀编委

王寿宴　张　钢　张复信　王振民　孙雨田　徐思民　耿龙武

组织委员会

主　任：许夕华

副主任：陈　奕　史俊棠

委　员：沈华菊　谈友娟　潘　晴

编辑委员会

主　任：谈志坚

副主任：谈　珂

主　编：孙冬宁

执行副主编：王　晶

副主编：梁　冰　李义勇　吕　焰　郭万保　何　梁　朱相欣

委　员：石军良　朱宏轩　崔　峰　杨　勇　张传富　李　波

The Intangible Cultural Heritage File

China Time-honored Brand·Yixing Baking Crafts of Yixing Goldfish Purple Ceramic Wine Bottle

Invited Editor

Wang Shouyan, Zhang Gang, Zhang Fuxin, Wang Zhenmin, Sun Yutian, Xu Simin, Geng Longwu

Organizing Committee

Director : Xu Xihua

Deputy Director : Chen Yi, Shi Juntang

Members : Shen Huaju, Tan Youjuan, Pan Qing

Editorial Board

Director : Tan Zhijian

Deputy Director : Tan Ke

Editor-in-Chief : Sun Dongning

Executive Associate Editor : Wang Jing

Sub-editors : Liang Bing, Li Yiyong, Lv Yan, Guo Wanbao, He Liang, Zhu Xiangxin

Members : Shi Junliang, Zhu Hongxuan, Cui Feng, Yang Yong, Zhang Chuanfu, Li Bo

非 物 质 文 化 遗 产 档 案

中华老字号·传统技艺

The Intangible Cultural Heritage File

China Time-honored Brand · Traditional Techniques

目录 CONTENTS

山東非物質文化遺產研究中心
Shandong Intangible Cultural Heritage Research Center
老字号文化遗产研究专家
http://www.sdich.com

前言

在历史的浩瀚长河中，中华民族创造了光辉灿烂、丰富多彩的文化遗产，既有物质形态的“有形”文化遗产，又有主要通过“口传心授”的方式传承下来、以非物质形态存在的非物质文化遗产，蕴涵着丰富的历史资源、文化资源、经济资源、教育资源、科学资源，是各民族传统文化的珍贵记忆，充分表现了中华民族在历史进程中逐步形成的优秀文化价值观念和审美理念，凝聚着中华民族的深层文化基因，体现了中华民族充沛的文化创造力，对于人类的生存与发展具有独特价值与深远意义。

在众多的中国非物质文化遗产种类和类型中，传统技艺成为其中的重要组成部分。“技”表达的是技能、是工巧，是改造改善自然之物的力量和技术；“艺”表达的是法则，是秩序，是心智，是塑造应用之物的智慧和美术。技艺把实用与艺术、把共性和个性有机地融为一体，它所遵循的工艺、材料、技巧、程序、塑造的器用，传承着人类宝贵的智慧、情感、规则和审美的种种感悟和成果，为我们展示了千姿百态的文化物品和文化品格，让我们体察到文化的丰富性和人类才智的无限性。千百年来，传统技艺形成了完整而发达的手工生产体系，涉及人类生产实践和生活需要的各个领域，形成了诸如印刷、酿造、榨取、烹饪、炮制、木作、雕琢、烧造、冶炼、纺织、印染、刺绣、编结等难以尽数的专门技艺、技巧和知识。国务院已公布的1028项非物质文化遗产项目中，传统技艺类项目有186项，在各省（区、市）公布的4155项非物质文化遗产项目中，传统技艺类项目占到720项。2009年2月，文化部还举办了中国非物质文化遗产传统技艺大展系列活动，传统技艺类非物质文化遗产保护与可持续发展进入了新的阶段，取得了新的成就，为推动文化大发展大繁荣，满足人民群众的文化需求，促进社会主义和谐社会建设，发挥了重要作用。

与传统技艺异曲同工，“老字号”作为中华商业文化的精髓，凝聚了一代代中华儿女的心血和智慧，衍化成各地风土文化的象征和符号，成为一个区域乃至中华民族文化与情感的重要载体。以手工生产方式为基础的中国传统技艺，大多存在于各行业的“中华老字号”之中，一个或数个自主开发的传统技艺，成为支撑百年老店长盛不衰的关键。传统技艺以老字号为平台，老字号以传统技艺为支柱，共同发挥着记载历史、传承文明的重要作用，彰显着中华文明独特精神品格和民族气质，凝聚了中华造物技术思想和实践经验。老字号不仅掌握了行业内手工技艺的最高水平，还网罗了最具成就的传统技艺传承人，形成了世代相沿的产品、技艺和服务体系，为传统技艺营造了繁荣发展、因袭传承的家园，创造、继承和发展了优秀的民族文化。

在全球化、城市化和工业化进程中，我国的非物质文化遗产包括传统技艺，无时无刻不在受到严重冲击，其生存环境发生了急剧变化。许多非物质文化遗产受到掠夺性开发，一些传统技艺传承后继乏人。老字号现状也不容乐观，新中国成立初期，老字号大约有8000家，现在仅存一千多家，且经营困难举步维艰。如何从传统技艺和老字号入手，找到两者互相促进和推动的契合点，创新传统技艺保护和老字号振兴的有效举措，成为许多人的思考和探索方向。

近年来，山东非物质文化遗产研究中心创建了国内首个老字号文化遗产研究专业委员会，建设了一批非物质文化遗产研究基地，将“非物质文化遗产档案·中华老字号·传统技艺”申报列入国家社会科学基金艺术学重点立项项目，并出版了一系列著作，组织了一批专业化、职业化、专家化的非物质文化遗产保护和研究队伍。尤其是山东非物质文化遗产研究中心的一批青年学者始终关注老字号非物质文化遗产的挖掘保护和利用，默默从事“老字号文化遗产”传统技艺的研究和保护工作。他们不为书斋所困，活跃于非物质文化遗产第一线，通过艰苦的田野考察活动，利用现代设计理念和传媒手段，取得了大量宝贵的一手资料，与老字号单位一起，为传统技艺的保存、保护、传播和发展做了大量基础性和创新性的工作，并与非物质文化遗产申报和保护结合在一起，为老字号单位继往开来、持续发展发现了新的增长点，开创了融传统技艺和老字号于一体的非遗保护开发这一山东模式，对推动老字号单位经营发展和文化建设做出了应有努力。

“非物质文化遗产档案·中华老字号·传统技艺”系列图书基于国家社会科学基金艺术学课题项目，从传统技艺、代表传承人、民俗文化等方面的田野考察为基本线索，对老字号单位中的传统技艺进行了系统的挖掘整理，采用大量图表、照片与影像资料，翔实介绍了各省非物质文化遗产中“老字号”类传统技艺项目的悠久历史和发展现状，展示了与当地经济发展、文化传统的紧密关系，以及在老百姓日常生活中的意义与作用，表现出传统技艺独特的历史、文化、精神、科学、教育和审美价值，是保护、发展传统技艺和老字号单位的创新性举措和历史性贡献。

本图书系列的编辑出版不仅对于保护老字号文化遗产的传统技艺提供了一个个有说服力的个案分析，还启发我们对于今天仍然作为生产、生活方式存在而不可分离的非物质文化遗产，应采取多种手段加以积极的生态型（性）和生产性传承保护，为传统技艺乃至其他类型非物质文化遗产的保护与发展营造良好环境，形成富有活力、独具特色的工作体系和工作方式。从这个意义上讲，本项目（图书）系列更有其启示、借鉴和示范作用。

愿更多有识之士以传承和保护非物质文化遗产为己任，热情参与到非物质文化遗产保护工作队伍中来，为我国非物质文化遗产保护事业作出更多更大的贡献。

马盛德

中华人民共和国文化部非物质文化遗产司副司长　马盛德

2009年10月29日

前言

PREFACE

In the vast river of the history, Chinese Nation created a brilliant, rich and colorful cultural heritage. There are both material shape of the "tangible" cultural heritage, and non-material form of existence of Non-material cultural heritage which mainly handed down through "Teach and learn by mouth and heart " method. These non-material cultural heritages containing rich historical resources, cultural resources, economical resources, educational resources, scientific resources, are precious memories of the national traditional culture, fully demonstrated the Chinese nation in the historical process of the gradual formation of the outstanding cultural values and aesthetic ideals, embody the Chinese nation's deep cultural genes, reflect the Chinese people with plenty of cultural creativities. Have unique value and far-reaching significance for human survival and development.

Among lots of categories and types of China's intangible cultural heritages, the traditional arts become one of the important component. "Technical" expresses skills, it is the strength and techniques of transforming and improving the natural compounds. "Art" expresses the laws, is mental, is the wisdom of shaping the application objects. Techniques organically integrated the practical and artistic, the general character and individuality into one. The use of technologies, materials, techniques, procedures and shaping which it followed inherited all kinds of insights and results of valuable human wisdom, emotions, rules and aesthetic, showed us different attitudes of cultural goods and cultural character, let us understand the richness of culture and the infinite nature of human intelligence. For thousands of years, traditional techniques formed a complete and well-developed manual production systems, related production practices and daily life of human needs in various fields, formed countless specialized techniques, skills and knowledge such as printing, brewing, squeezing, cooking, concocting, carpentry, carving, firing, smelting, textile, printing and dyeing, embroidery, knitting and so on. Among the 1028 intangible cultural heritage projects announced by the State Council, there are 186 projects are Traditional Techniques. Among 4155 intangible cultural heritage projects published by provinces (autonomous regions and municipalities), the traditional arts categories of projects accounted for 720. In February 2009, China Ministry of Culture has held a series of activities of traditional art exhibition of China's intangible cultural heritage. Intangible cultural heritage protection and sustainable development has entered a new phase, new achievements. It has played an important role to promote cultural development great prosperity, to meet the cultural needs of the people, and promote the building of a harmonious socialist society.

Similar to the traditional techniques, as the essence of the Chinese business culture, "time-honored brand" embodies efforts and wisdom of the generations of Chinese descendants, evolved into a symbol and symbols of the customs and culture, and becoming an important carrier of culture and emotion in a region and even the Chinese nation. Based on manual production mode, traditional Chinese techniques, most exist in various sectors of the "China time-honored". One or several self-developed traditional techniques and art has become the key to enduring support of century-old store. Time-honored brand as a platform of traditional techniques, traditional techniques as a pillar of the time-honored brand. They both play an important role of recording history and spreading civilization, highlighting the unique spiritual character of Chinese culture and national temperament, agglomerating the Chinese thought of creation techniques and practical experience. Time-honored brand not only mastered the industry's highest level of manual skill, but also gathers the most accomplished Inheritances. They formed products, skills and service system from generation to generation, create homes of prosperity and development for the traditional skills, create, inherit and develop the excellent national culture.

During the process of globalization, urbanization and industrialization, China's intangible cultural heritage, including traditional techniques, at all times, facing a serious impact, their living environment has undergone dramatic changes. Many intangible cultural heritages were overexploited, some of the traditional techniques heritages are lack of inheritance. Status quo of time-honored brand can not be optimistic, either. On the early days, there were about 8000 brands, but now, there are only about 1000 remaining, and also under a difficult operating condition. How can we start from traditional techniques and time-honored brand, to find the meeting point of promote and facilitate of the two factors, to innovate traditional techniques protection and effectively revitalize the time-honored brand, now become many people's exploration direction.

In recent years, Shandong Intangible Cultural Heritage Research Center founded the first "Time-honored Brand" Cultural Heritage Studies Committee in China. And built a batch of intangible cultural heritage research bases. Declared and Listed "Intangible Cultural Heritage Files · China Time-honored Brand · Traditional Craft" in the key project of arts in National Social Science Fund. And published series of books.Organized a group of professional, career-oriented, expert-oriented intangible cultural heritage protection and research teams. Especially a group of young scholars of the Intangible Cultural Heritage Research Center of Shandong Province has always been concerned about the mining protection and use of the intangible cultural heritage of Time-honored Brand companies. quiet and engaged in research and protection work of "Time-honored Brand cultural heritage". They are not trapped in books, working actively in the first line of the intangible cultural heritage, through the arduous field trips, use of modern design concepts and media, and gained valuable first-hand information. Together with the "Time-honored Brand" enterprises, done a lot of basic and innovative work for the preservation, protection, dissemination and development of traditional techniques, and with the declaration and protection of intangible cultural heritage, combining the old and famous enterprises carried forward the sustainable development of the discovery of new growth points, creating a financial skills and "Time-honored Brand" tradition development in one of the non-legacy mode of protection and development of Shandong, to promote the "Time-honored Brand" business development and cultural development and make its due efforts.

The book series of "Intangible Cultural Heritage Files · China Time-honored Brand · Traditional Craft " are based on the Key Project of of Art Science of National Social Science. Use the traditional techniques, representative inheritances, folk customs and cultural aspects of the field trips as the basic clue to Traditional techniques of the "Time-honored Brand" enterprise for a systematic excavation of finishing, using a large number of charts, photographs and video data, Informative introduction to the history and current situation of the development of the project of " Time-honored Brand " traditional craft of provincial intangible cultural heritage, demonstrating with the local economic development and cultural tradition of close ties, as well as the people the meaning and role of everyday life, showing traditional skills unique historical, cultural, spiritual, scientific, educational and aesthetic value, is to protect and develop the traditional techniques and "Time-honored Brand" companies and innovative initiatives and historical contributions.

The purpose of editing and publishing this book series, not only for the protection of cultural heritage, traditional techniques which have provided a convincing case study, but also inspired us when facing intangible cultural heritage that are still existed as productivity, way of life is not separable, should be adopt various means to be an active and productive eco-heritage protection for the traditional techniques as well as other types of intangible cultural heritage protection and development to create a good environment for the formation of a dynamic, unique work system and work style. In this sense, the book series have their inspiration, drawing, and exemplary role.

In order to pass responsibility and the protection of intangible cultural heritage, we hope more insight people of passion participate in the protection of intangible cultural heritage ranks for the cause of protecting China's intangible cultural heritage to make more and greater contributions.

Ma Shengde

Deputy Director-General of the Department of the Intangible Cultural Heritage,

Ministry of Culture of the People's Republic of China

29th Oct,2009

总序

General Preface

中华老字号

谈「非遗」语境下的「老字号文化遗产」生态保护

谈“非遗”语境下的“老字号文化遗产”生态保护

“非遗”保护的机遇与挑战

中国的非物质文化遗产是中华文明的重要组成部分，保护好非物质文化遗产，是历史赋予我们的责任。当前我国社会正处于全面建设小康社会的重要战略机遇期，保护非物质文化遗产，对于增强民族自信心、自豪感，增强民族认同感、归属感，促进经济、社会、文化的全面协调发展，构建社会主义和谐社会，都将起到积极的促进作用。

近年来，我国非物质文化遗产保护作为国策得到国家的重视，建立了系统的非物质文化遗产保护机制和运作程序，一批非物质文化遗产项目和传承人已经或正在被挖掘保护，非物质文化遗产项目的开发与创新总体向好，许多非物质文化遗产保护和研究组织和专业化、专家化人才队伍日益壮大，民间非物质文化遗产保护意识和氛围日渐浓厚，群众化基础不断稳固。保护工作正成为国家发展战略的重要组成部分，与构建和谐社会相适应，从被动保护向主动保护，从单一保护向全面保护，从静态保护向“活态”整体性保护转变，非物质文化遗产保护与开发利用呈现一派新的气象，焕发出勃勃生机，进入一个全新的发展机遇期。但从另一方面也应看到，受历史上种种时间和空间条件限制以及现代文明的冲击，我国历史上许多曾经鲜活的非物质文化形态变得了无生机，成了“病树”，而恰恰是这些“病树”，曾经、正在并将继续见证中国文化的沧桑与博大，这使我国非物质文化遗产保护工作面临严峻的形势和挑战：非物质文化遗产生存的文化生态环境急剧改变，资源流失状况严重，一些传统技艺面临灭绝；非物质文化遗产还没有得到依法保护，法律法规建设有待加快步伐；非物质文化遗产保护意识有待提高；保护机制有待进一步完善。

“非遗”保护的文化语境

从中国传统文化层面看，中华民族非物质文化是先民们博大智慧的结晶，尽管它主要产生于民间，但与其他物质或精神文化遗产一样，与中国传统文化密不可分。研究中国非物质文化，一个绕不过去的课题便是它与中国传统文化的渊源。传统文化基因已经深深根植于中国人的文化血液中，即便春秋以前的非物质文化也与传统文化同质。因此，任何对中国非物质文化的研究必须置身于中国传统文化语境中。

从文化交流层面看，任何一种文化在与自身之外的文化交流的过程中，往往呈现为通约性与不可通约性并行的状态。换言之，世界上所有文化以丰富多彩的形式共同构成世界文化，同时均保持着自身文化的独立性，有着自身鲜明的文化个性与文化语境，非物质文化亦然。随着我国综合国力的提升，近几年“国学”复苏，中国传统文化以活跃的姿态挺进全球。民族复兴的脚步，也响彻在话语权的“抢夺战”中。事实证明，我们要推进的不仅仅是形而上的儒释道，包括非物质文化在内的中国传统文化在世界范围内的传播，通常需要具体的文化形态作为载体。我们来列举两个耳熟能详的例子，如功夫和中医。功夫和中医在西方的传播盛行，背后彰显的就是中国传统文化。

从传承创新层面看，中国非物质文化博大精深，活力充沛。我们不能仅仅局限于对非物质文化的保护，保护也是为了传承。我们对非物质文化的保护必须与本土化现代艺术设计、本土文化产业等结合起来。在对非物质文化的吸收、扬弃与变革中加以继承。那种把非物质文化放到“静态保护”状态，使其充当所谓文明进程活化石的想法是幼稚的。因为，我们必须正视的一个事实就是：现代化已经无孔不入。非物质文化区域内的个体（主要指非物质文化传承者）也有享受现代化成果的愿望和权利。在文化产业或创意产业中，我们应当在立足于自身的民族文化的基础上，锐意创新，根据时代特征，将本土非物质文化放到动态创新层面，置于活态发展空间，使非物质文化遗产的继承与发展充满生机与活力。

“老字号”的“非遗”特质

“老字号”作为特指的经济文化现象，成为历代经济文化繁荣的标志，它以斋、坊、铺、堂的形式成为有形的物质文化遗产，但也以特有的经营理念、手工技艺和服务策略成为无形的非物质文化遗产，“老字号”品牌是其所属的非物质文化遗产最集中的物质化体现，具有深远的历史渊源和厚重的文化底蕴。“老字号”所属的传统技艺与中国传统文化的基本理念、价值取向、功能结构以及品质形态紧密相连，与人类日常生活欲求心理及社会文明教化密切相关，比较典型地体现了中华传统文化的内涵和特征。甚至可以说，它既是中华文化理念的表现形式，又是中华文化精神生生不息的传播媒介。传统技艺总是与地域文化紧密联系，显示出各个地区各个时期的特色物产、乡土风气、人情习性、行为劳作等各个方面的特征，是中国民间文化的物化形态，其所包含的饮食思想、制作工艺、传播习俗暗合科学，是中国传统文化中的精粹，其所传递和继承的深刻的人文精神、达观的人生态度和淳厚的乡土风俗，有其独特的文化价值，体现了中华民族的独创精神，展示出珍贵的历史价值、科学价值、人文价值、民俗价值、经济价值及社会价值，承载着丰富的历史、文化和民俗信息，成为宝贵的非物质文化遗产。

按照胡锦涛同志“要拥有我们自己的核心技术，要拥有我们民族的世界品牌”的要求，在抢救、保护、传承、发展的基础上，应倍加珍惜“老字号”的品牌价值，努力寻求传统特色与现代元素的融合点，创新老字号品牌，在保护传承原有独特技艺的基础上积极应用现代科技和传播方式，在开拓创新中展示浓郁地方特色，传承独具匠心的传统技艺和服务，将凝聚世代先辈的心血和智慧、体现诚信经营的商业文化精髓发扬光大，为弘扬中华文明和和谐社会建设服务。

融合传统技艺与老字号的“非遗”保护模式

中华大地有着古老的文化积淀和丰富的文化传承，在民间留存有大量鲜活的、源自劳动人民的传统技艺。历代老百姓以其智慧、热情和技巧，创造了源远流长、千姿百态、人情浓厚的民间各种门类传统技艺。作为非物质文化遗产重要组成部分的传统技艺业——东阿镇福牌阿胶、宜兴紫砂金鱼陶瓷酒瓶、周村烧饼、王村醋、潍坊红木嵌银漆器、龙口粉丝、崔字香油、义兴张道口烧鸡、玉堂酱园、宜兴紫砂范家壶庄、景芝酒、古贝春酒、即墨老酒、鲁菜、青州隆盛糕点、鲁东铜响乐器、乾隆杯酒等等老字号类传统技艺的生产性保护，无疑为中国非物质文化遗产保护与传承提供了一种新颖的视角，而在这种生产性保护中，保护和研究者对于历史文化的挖掘工作又是令人感动的。换言之，对于上述非物质文化的传承与保护是置身于中国文化和现代化语境之内的。我们应当从中国传统文化内涵、审美、文化心理以及置身于中国文化语境之内的非物质文化社会学、产业经济学角度探讨中国非物质文化的传承。所以，从老字号入手挖掘和开发传统技艺，积极开展非物质文化遗产保护和研究工作，不失为一种可资商榷的新思路。

通过对各地非物质文化遗产的田野调查发现，各地的民间文学、美术、音乐、戏曲、曲艺、舞蹈等非物质文化遗产的研究已经做得非常翔实。但由于各种原因，目前可见的文献中，对传统技艺的学术研究尚不充分，成形的科研考察资料就更少，甚至图像资料的收集都不甚完整，且分散于各地方的文化研究机构。由于全球化背景下的中华文明正处于转型期，非物质文化遗产的教育传承在各地方大学教育和研究的发展刚刚起步，因此，注重发挥非物质文化遗产所在区域的研究机构和人员作用，对本地非物质文化遗产资源进行全面的普查、收集、记录和研究，对传统技艺以及与之相关的民俗文化进行系统的考察与整理，更具有历史与现实意义。

山东非物质文化遗产研究中心集中力量开展的中华老字号文化遗产研究，并编撰出版“非物质文化遗产档案·中华老字号·传统技艺”系列图书，就是在这一背景下的探索和努力。希望通过这一工作，为传统技艺和老字号的保护和发展聊尽绵薄之力，为后人留下“非遗”保护工作的档案袋和资料夹。果能如此，则幸甚至哉。

《非物质文化遗产档案·中华老字号·传统技艺》 编委会

2009年10月1日 国庆节

A Discussion on "Time-honored Brand Cultural Heritage" Ecological Protection under Intangible Cultural Heritage Background

Challenges and opportunities of protecting Intangible Cultural Heritage

Intangible Cultural Heritage is an important component of Chinese civilization, so it is our responsibility to protect Intangible Heritage. At present, China is in a critical strategic phase toward to building well-off society on all-around way, therefore, protecting Intangible Cultural Heritage will enhance the national confidence and pride, improve the national identification and sense of belonging, drive all-around harmonious development of the economy, society and culture, and build harmonious society of socialism actively.

In recent years, as part of a national policy, our country's Intangible Cultural Heritage protection effort has attracted high degree attention by the government, and systematic procedures and systems on protecting Intangible Cultural Heritage has been established. A series of Intangible Cultural Heritage projects and inheritors have been and are being protected. The overall trend of the development and innovation of Intangible Cultural Heritage is well on track and many Intangible Cultural Heritage protecting and study organizations as well as specialized talents has emerged and boomed. Intangible Cultural Heritage protection has been rooted deeply among the whole society. So the protection of Intangible Cultural Heritage has become an important part of our country's development strategy. In line with the effort to build a harmonious society, the protection work has turned from passive to active, from partial to whole, from static to dynamic, and the Intangible Cultural Heritage protection work has taken on a new look with energetic life and has come to a new development era with numerous opportunities. On the other hand, however, we should also notice that, due to various time and spacial restrictions as well as the impact of modern civilizations, some Intangible Cultural Heritage that once full of life in the past now turns lifeless, making people think they are just like ill trees, and it's just these ill trees that were, are and will testify the broad and deeply-rooted Chinese culture.

Now, the protection effort of Intangible Cultural Heritage in China is facing with severe situation: first, cultural environment for the survival of Intangible Cultural Heritage changes dramatically, resources are lost seriously, and some traditional workmanships are facing the fact of die-out; And, second, Intangible Cultural Heritage has not been protected by laws, so the establishment of law and regulation system has to be accelerated ; third, the awareness for protecting Intangible Cultural Heritage needs to be enhanced; and fourth, the protection system should be improved.

The culture background of Intangible Cultural Heritage protection

From the perspective of Chinese traditional culture, Chinese Intangible Cultural Heritage is the result of broad wisdom of our ancestors. Though they come from the public, they are closely related with Chinese traditional culture, like other material or mental cultural heritage. An unavoidable topic for studying Chinese Intangible Cultural Heritage is the relationship with Chinese traditional culture. Traditional culture gene has been rooted deeply in cultural blood of Chinese, even Intangible Cultural Heritage before the Spring and Autumn Period is consubstantial with traditional culture. Hence, any study on Chinese Intangible Cultural Heritage must be rooted in Chinese traditional culture context.

From the perspective of cultural exchange, the commensurability and incommensurability are usually coexisting during the exchange of any culture with foreign one. In other words, all cultures in the world form the universal culture in various ways, and each maintain its own independence with unique cultural feature and context, so does Intangible Cultural Heritage. With the enhancement of comprehensive national power of China and the renaissance of Chinese Culture in recent years, Chinese traditional culture is being popular in the world. The step of national renaissance is also rending in the battle for the speech right. The fact shows that we should not only promote metaphysical Ru-Shi-Dao, the promulgation of Chinese traditional culture including Intangible Cultural Heritage usually requires concrete cultural form as the barrier. For example, the popularity of Chinese Kungfu and Traditional Chinese Medicine in west countries demonstrates the power of Chinese traditional culture.

From the perspective of the heritance and innovation, Chinese Intangible Cultural Heritage is deeply rooted and dynamic. We should not only limit the protection of Intangible Cultural Heritage, but also pass down it. The protection of Intangible Cultural Heritage must be correlated with local modern art design and local culture industry. We should inherit Intangible Cultural Heritage while absorbing, developing, discarding and changing it. It is unwise to place Intangible Heritage in “static” state and make it the living fossil of the civilization process. One fact that we must envisage is: the modernization is ubiquitous. Individuals in Intangible Cultural Heritage area (mainly the inheritor of Intangible Heritage) have the willing and right of enjoying modern culture results. In the culture industry or creative industry, we should innovate local Intangible Cultural Heritage dynamically according to the characteristics of our times on basis of our national culture in order to give it a dynamic development environment, making the inheritance and development of Intangible Cultural Heritage full of life.

The unique attributes of Time-Honored Brand as Intangible Cultural Heritage

As specific economic and cultural phenomena, “Time-honored Brands” become the symbol of economic and cultural prosperity in the history. They are tangible cultural heritage in the form of Room, Workshop, Store and Hall, but they are also intangible Intangible Cultural Heritage with unique business concept, handcraft and service strategy. “Time-honored Brands” is the most collective material reflection of Intangible Cultural Heritage, and carries profound history and rich cultural significance. Traditional handcraft of “Time-honored Brand” is closely related to basic concept, value proposition, functional structure and quality of Chinese traditional culture, and to desire mentality of daily life and social civilization, and typically represents the significance and characteristics of Chinese traditional culture. In fact, it is the expression form of Chinese culture concept, and is the promulgation medium of Chinese cultural spirit. Traditional handcraft is usually related to regional culture to reflect unique product, native climate, human relationship and behavior of each region in each period. It is the material state of Chinese folk culture. The food concept, production technique and promulgation habit contained in it accords with scientific idea, and reflects the essence of Chinese traditional culture. The profound human spirit, optimistic attitude and pure native habit it transmits and passes down have unique cultural value, and reflect creative spirit of Chinese nation. It has precious historical, scientific, cultural, folk custom, economical and social value and carries abundant historical, cultural and folk custom information as precious Intangible Cultural Heritages.

As called on by Hu Jintao, “We should have our own core technology, and we should have world brand of our nation”, we should value the value of “Time-honored Brands” while saving, protecting, passing down and developing them, seek for the convergence point between traditional features and modern elements, innovate these time-honored brands, utilize modern technology and promulgation mode on basis of protecting and passing down original unique techniques, demonstrate rich local features during the innovation, pass down unique traditional technique and service, and carry forward the business culture essence which concentrates the painstaking effort and wisdom of ancestor and reflects honest business approach, so as to make a contribution to promoting Chinese civilization and building harmonious society.

The Intangible Cultural Heritage protection method of combining traditional handicraft with Time-honored brand

There are massive ancient cultural deposition and rich cultural heritages on the land of China, and there are a large number of living traditional handcraft techniques here. With their wisdom, passion and technique, people here create various long-established and rich traditional handcraft techniques. As an important part of Intangible Cultural Heritage, the protection of traditional handcraft industry – Dong'e Town Fu Brand Donkey-hide Gelatin, Yixing Goldfish Purple Ceramic Wine Bottle, Zhoucun Griddle Cake, Wangcun Vinegar, Weifang Redwood Silver-inlaying Lacquer, Longkou Vermicelli, Cui Brand Balsam, Daokou Yi Xing Zhang Brand Roast Chicken, Yutang Sauce, Yixing Fanjiahuzhuang Brand Purple Sand Pot, Jingzhi Wine, Gubeichun Wine, Jimo Old Wine, Shandng Dishes, Qingzhou Longsheng Brnd Pastry, Brass Instrument in East Shandong, Qianlongbei Wine, etc. provides a new angle of view for the protection and inheritance of Chinese Intangible Cultural Heritage. In such productive protection process, we are deeply impressed with the history and culture discovery effort made by the protectors and researchers. In other words, the inheritance and protection of above Intangible Cultural Heritages are performed in Chinese culture and modern context. Therefore, we should discuss the inheritance of Chinese Intangible Cultural Heritage from the perspective of Chinese traditional culture significance, aesthetics, cultural psychology, as well as sociology and industry economics of Intangible Cultural Heritage in Chinese culture context. So, you can see, it's a feasible and new way to carry out Intangible Heritage protection and research work by exploring and developing traditional handicraft based on the Time-honored brands.

The field survey throughout the country on Intangible Cultural Heritage finds that many predecessors have studied these heritages like folk fine arts, music, drama, traditional art, etc. However, academic study on traditional crafts is not sufficient in available documents, even the picture materials are not collected completely, and they are dispersed in local culture research organizations. At present, Chinese civilization is in a transition period under the globalization environment, the education and study on Intangible Cultural Heritage is just beginning in local universities and research institutions. Therefore, it will be historically and realistically significant for regional research center where cultural heritage is located to survey, collect, record and research local Intangible Cultural Heritage, and to review and organize traditional crafts and the related folk culture systematically.

It's under this background that Shandong Intangible Cultural Heritage Research Center put great efforts on the cultural heritage research of time-honored brands and compile and publish the series of books 《Intangible Cultural Heritage Files · China Time-honored Brand · Traditional Craft》. We hope our work will make some contribution to the protection and development of Chinese traditional handicraft and Chinese time-honored brands and leave valuable information on protection of Intangible Cultural Heritages for our posterity.

The Editorial Board on Intangible Cultural Heritage Files · China Time-honored Brand · Traditional Crafts

1st Oct,2009

序

General Preface

中华老字号

传承与创新的成功范例

传承与创新的成功范例

近年来，金鱼陶瓷有限公司大力加强企业文化建设，以公司传承与创新宜兴地域陶瓷文化为抓手，进行了大量挖掘、整理和研究工作，展示了公司兴盛与发展的软实力，更对宜兴陶瓷经济与文化发展注入了新的活力。作为一项重要成果，《宜兴金鱼紫砂陶瓷酒瓶烧造技艺》一书即将付梓，谈志坚董事长请我作序，我自觉水平有限却又欣然应允。一是因为我与谈董共事多年，爱陶瓷、爱宜兴成为我们共同的信念与追求。二是因为研究与弘扬宜兴陶瓷文化本就是行业协会之职责，对于紫砂文化和这几年声名鹊起的金鱼陶瓷酒瓶，还真有许多话要说。

宜兴素有“陶都”美誉，有着7000年制陶史，精陶、彩陶、均陶、青瓷、紫砂“五朵金花”在世界独树一帜。尤其是令世人瞩目的紫砂，已成为陶都宜兴的标志。紫砂，始于北宋，盛于明、清，是用宜兴独有的一种质地细腻、含铁量高的特殊陶土，以传统工艺制成的无釉细陶，有茶具、酒具、花盆及雕塑等品种，造型多样，色泽雅致。尤其是紫砂壶艺，融合历史悠久的陶文化与成熟于唐代的茶文化，在数百年的薪火相传中，注入了历代文人气息和艺人制陶技艺精髓，“冠绝一世，独步千秋”，成为无与伦比的陶中瑰宝。

中国产陶，历史悠久，《周书》里有“神宜耕而作陶”，《路史》里有“燧人范金合土为釜”。早在六千五百年前，宜兴地区就开始生产陶器，历经各个历史时期从未中断，有着深厚的陶文化底蕴。延至宋代，随着茶文化的兴盛发展，宜兴陶瓷艺人利用本地陶土资源开始生产紫砂陶，并逐步发展成为一门有着独特艺术语言的，令全世瞩目的陶瓷艺术门类。宋代诗人欧阳修、梅尧臣等的诗作中，也都有关于紫砂茶具的诗句。1976年，蠡墅羊角山发掘出一座宋代紫砂古龙窑遗址及大量早期紫砂残品的堆积层，发现了壶、罐两大类紫砂陶遗迹。明嘉靖至万历年间，是宜兴紫砂的成熟时期，先有董翰、赵梁、元畅、时鹏“四大家”，继有时大彬、李仲芳、徐友泉“三大家”。槌片、围圈、打身筒的成型法和泥片镶接成型法渐趋完善。明末至清代，为紫砂工艺的繁荣时期。紫砂工艺向装饰纹样，花样图案造型发展，出现了许多技巧精细、形象完善、结构纤密的砂器瑰宝。近代和现代，宜兴紫砂到达鼎盛时期，从泥料质地到工艺流程，从紫砂科研到流派创新都有新的发展，据1919年的有关资料记载，当时宜兴的蜀山、丁山、汤渡和川埠一带的沿山居民，“家家制坯，户户捶泥”。新中国成立后，紫砂的生产品种从紫砂壶和花盆等数种发展到上百种，大量艺人精于壶艺、书画、雕刻、花盆造型以及雕塑艺术等，不仅精品与日俱增，还发展了书画雕刻和古今人物的紫砂雕塑作品。

经历代制陶艺人的发展，加以茶文化的融入，以及古代文人雅士对紫砂陶艺的推崇和参与，宜兴紫砂历尽三百多年的发展，创造了陶刻、镶嵌（镶嵌金、银、玉石、色泥、螺钿、红木、瓷花等）、包锡、包漆、泥绘、粉彩、彩釉、珐琅彩、描余、浮雕、镂雕、绞泥、模印、贴饰等一系列装饰技艺。其中最具代表性的是陶刻，它是诗文、金石、书画、篆刻艺术与紫砂制作技艺的完美结合，深符中华民族传统的审美标准，尤与文人阶层的审美情趣相吻合。优美无匹的紫砂土与江南山水的灵气，培育了一代代紫砂艺人，诞生出千姿百态的紫砂艺术品，以其文化气息和艺术高度，成为文化与艺术的共有载体，为中华民族传统文化，为世界艺术文化之旅竖起了一座座里程碑。

紫砂壶自是为世人所熟知，岂不知宜兴也一直有以紫砂做酒器的传统。紫砂酒器中有温酒器、盛酒器和饮酒器等，有各种造型的酒壶、酒杯，南京博物院收藏项圣思蟠桃形紫砂杯，胎质细腻，色泽红润，即出自宜兴窑。酒器既盛装琼浆玉液，又传播文化和历史，它集酒艺、酒史、陶艺、瓷艺、绘画、书法、诗词、雕刻、民俗等为一体，是一种特殊的工艺品。据文字记载，新石器文化时期就出现了形状类似后世酒器的陶器、牛角器以及商周时期的青铜酒器。在长江下游的浙江余姚河姆渡文化遗址中，曾出土与饮酿行为有密切关系的陶鬲、陶盉等器物，有些学者判定为中国目前发现最早的酒具。在属于大汶口文化的大范庄遗址中，酒器占出土陶器的百分之九十以上。新石器时代至夏代，以陶酒器为主，铜、漆酒器为辅；秦汉时期以漆酒器为主，铜、玉酒器次之；魏晋时期以瓷酒器为主，玉酒器次之；唐宋至明清时期仍然以瓷酒器最为流行，元、明、清时代的梅瓶就是当时盛酒瓷器中的一种。从魏晋到唐宋明清时期，瓷酒具一直稳坐霸主宝座。明清时期是中国陶瓷业发展的鼎盛时期，明代常见的酒具有玉壶春瓶、梨形壶、龙柄壶、梅瓶、鸡心壶、天球壶等。在装饰手法上有青花、釉里红、白釉、青釉、朱红釉等。工艺技术有彩绘、刻划、镂空、瓜瓣、模印、脱胎等。清代造型更为丰富，品种也越发多种多样，如倒流壶、温酒壶等。

宜兴陶瓷酒器的发展历程，大体与我国酒器发展史相对应。但也具有其独到的特点。一是源远流长，从新石器文化肇始，历经数千年，从红陶、硬陶、原始青瓷，再到紫砂工艺陶、现代青瓷，宜兴陶瓷火种历久不熄。二是民用为主，酒器产品多为人们生活日用品，少有贡品御器之类的精致代表作，与水具、茶具相比而言，专制、专用的特别体现并不十分突出。三是原料多样，瓷土、陶土、紫砂泥等，都被广泛用来烧陶制瓷。在宜兴陶土资源开发利用的各个不同时期，矿源开采、泥料炼制的工艺不断更新提高，具有广泛的适应性、实用性和多样性，即便是紫砂陶这一概念性的提法，也不足千年。四是因地因时制宜，当地陶土资源丰富、外地瓷土流量不足时，以本地陶土、陶泥为主要原料；紫砂茶具升值、瓷土交易便捷时，则以瓷质酒具为主。五是善于继承和创新，瓷胎与紫砂色、紫砂胎与色釉有机结合，各种紫砂陶瓷酒瓶应世而生，紫砂陶土价值与现代工艺价值同步显现，为弘扬紫砂陶瓷文化奏响厚重乐章。

宜兴紫砂陶瓷酒瓶融合宜兴陶瓷的厚重底蕴、紫砂文化的独特风韵，以及酒瓶文化艺术，追溯紫砂渊源，锤炼陶瓷风骨，因应酒具大势，赋以文化传承、技艺创新和繁荣经济的使命，集中展示了宜兴地域内生产生活方式、百姓共同特质和文化审美习惯的，体现出非物质文化遗产独特性、活态性、传承性、变异性、综合性和地域性等基本特点，是非物质文化遗产项目生产性方式保护、继承和创新的成功案例。可以这样说，中国酒文化的弘扬，让传统的陶艺文化新辟了展示其水平的舞台，反之，丰富多彩的中国陶文化，又提升了中国的酒文化。

从陶瓷烧造技艺的角度，区分陶与瓷最主要的条件是原材料和烧成温度。以高岭土作坯，烧成温度在陶器所需要的温度阶段，则为陶器，例如古代的白陶。高岭土在瓷器所需要的温度下，所制的坯体则成为瓷器。紫砂是介于瓷和陶之间的一种特殊物质，高龄土岩化到一定程度开始结晶成砂，也就是广义上的紫砂。高龄土经高温烧制后其结构呈晶体状排列，内部结构有序紧密，表面平整光洁，呈玻璃状，是为瓷器。经岩化后的高龄土成砂状结晶，烧成后的陶器内部呈鳞片状排列，鳞片之间形成链状气道，由于这个气道极小，加以水在大气压力下存在阻尼现象，就形成了透气而不渗水的紫砂。既透气又渗水的陶瓷则称之谓陶。在几千年陶瓷烧制中，常常可以看到紫砂的影子，古人对陶瓷器具的材质的选择不很精准，只是因地而异的一般粘土。六朝时期，在宜兴原始青瓷（釉陶）和施青釉的产品中，就出现了紫色胎，这种紫色胎与通常所见的陶胎不完全一样，从外观看，这种紫色胎土颜色和明清时期的紫砂胎较为接近，这说明紫砂与青瓷在原料利用方面异曲同工，紫砂器制作技艺应该在某些方面传承了青瓷烧造技艺的成果。唐初宜兴归径等地曾大量烧制青瓷，这时瓷器的胎质中已含有紫砂成分，说明古人已有意无意地运用了紫砂原料。

而随着科技的进步、生产力的提高在新工艺和材料方面的创新，紫砂原料在陶与瓷中均占有了相当位置，金鱼紫砂陶瓷酒瓶因而应运而生。它从材料筛选、研磨、选择先进的现代工艺设备等方面入手，采用了文片瓷（表面有裂纹）做酒瓶的技术，即在釉和胎之间加过渡层，为紫砂烧制与釉的烧制提供不同温度，从而解决了高温烧制紫砂器皿易开裂的的技术难题，消除了紫砂器皿所特有的渗漏缺陷，最终成功烧制出了紫砂陶瓷酒瓶，成为宜兴陶瓷家族的新宠。

在陶瓷烧造技艺领域，金鱼紫砂陶瓷酒瓶实现了紫砂矿物原料与陶瓷工艺性能的有机结合；在文化传承延续方面，它实现了传统技艺、大众习俗与地域特色文化的有机结合；在经营管理层面，它实现了文化艺术品与大众日用品的有机结合，从而使紫砂陶瓷酒瓶传统烧造技艺，以紫砂原料和陶瓷艺术结合度强、高档酒瓶与高档酒共生性强、工艺传承与技术创新凝合力强的特点，成为高档紫砂酒瓶创新领域的佼佼者，成为兼具紫砂文化意象、陶瓷工艺特征和高雅消费趣味的鲜明载体，在酒瓶文化发展中形成鲜明特色。

金鱼陶瓷有限公司的紫砂陶瓷酒瓶造型千姿百态，其人物造型优美典雅，动物造型惟妙惟肖，线条造型简洁明快，植物造型栩栩如生。其饰文化更是丰富多彩，有五彩缤纷的釉水，有似釉非釉的化妆土，有釉无釉相间的点彩，有粗犷雅丽的手彩，有形象逼真的浮雕，有张扬个性的色胎，有淳朴自然的喷砂，更有融书画为一体的镌刻，华贵富丽的镀膜，另有为酒厂量身打造的字画，商标、商标介绍的贴花装饰，均为天下独绝。紫砂陶瓷酒瓶以其富有内涵的外观和饱经风霜而形成地质地，淋漓尽致地展现了酒文化的博大精深，深受酿酒行业青睐，多年来，该公司始终保持了供不应求的销售强势，并成为行业的领头羊，更为传播紫砂文化作出了巨大贡献。

《宜兴金鱼紫砂陶瓷酒瓶烧造技艺》一书的出版，还得益于山东非物质文化遗产研究中心各位专家的辛勤努力。自2010年8月开始，专家组就在宜兴市丁蜀镇分民俗实物征集、行为采录和资料研究三个层面，进行田野调查。在调查过程中，以宜兴金鱼紫砂陶瓷酒瓶烧造技艺、代表传承人、民俗文化等方面为基本线索，归纳出宜兴金鱼紫砂陶瓷酒瓶烧造技艺的基本特征和核心元素，并进一步分析作为宜兴金鱼紫砂陶瓷酒瓶烧造技艺的稳定传承，及其在丁蜀镇、宜兴甚至江浙一带，直到整个中国的饮酒习俗和审美心理背后的文化特质、精神信仰等需求之间的联系，探求宜兴金鱼紫砂陶瓷酒瓶烧造技艺的深层规律和表现方式。重点对宜兴金鱼紫砂陶瓷酒瓶和与之相关的民俗文化进行了系统的考察与整理研究，揭示了这一制作工艺所具有的文化意义和非物质文化遗产的保护价值，对宜兴陶瓷文化研究做出了积极努力，取得了丰硕成果。在此，作为宜兴陶瓷文化的弘扬者，对山东同道表示衷心的感谢。

是为序。

中国陶瓷工业协会副理事长　史俊棠

2011年11月

A Successful Paradigm of Inheritance and Innovation

In recent years, Goldfish Ceramics Limited Company vigorously strengthen the building of enterprise culture. Grasp inheritance and innovation of Yixing regional ceramic culture, had a great deal mining, arrange and study, which shows the prosperity and development of soft power, and also injected new vitality to the Yixing ceramic culture and economic development. As an important outcome, “Baking Crafts of Yixing Goldfish Purple Ceramic Wine Bottle” is due out to be published. The chairman Tan Zhijian asked me make its preface, I perceived limited but embrace gladly. One is that I worked for many years with chairman Tan, love ceramic, love Yixing become our common belief and pursuit. Second is because the study and promotion of Yixing ceramic culture is the duty of the trade association. For the purple culture and Goldfish Ceramic Wine Bottle rise to fame these few years, I have many words to say.

Yixing was known as the reputation of "Pottery Capital". It has 7000 years history of ceramics making. The famous "Five Golden Flowers" including fine ceramics, Painted pottery, Jun pottery, Celadon and purple, are unique in the world. Especially the purple attracted worldwide attention, has become a symbol of "Pottery Capital"---Yi Xing. Purple, began in the Northern Song Dynasty and flourished in the Ming and Qing Dynasty, is a unique, special clay with delicate texture and high iron content in Yixing. The unglazed pottery made by traditional craft, have tea, wine, flower pots and sculpture and other species, shape varied, elegant color. In particular purple teapot art, Fusion ceramic culture with a long history and tea culture matured in the Tang Dynasty, Passing the torch in a few centuries, Injection of literati atmosphere and the essence of art pottery artists, "ranks first among the world, unmatched in future generations" , Become the incomparable pottery treasures.

Chinese ceramics has a long history. “Zhou History” read “Gods made pottery for cultivation”, “Lu Shi” read “ancient people cast metals and soil for kettle”. In the early 6,500 years ago, production of pottery were begun in Yixing area, and has never been interrupted after each historical period, has profound ceramic culture. Until the Song Dynasty, along with the flourishing development of tea culture, ceramic artists began produce purple pottery by using the local clay resources in Yixing, and gradually developed into a ceramic arts of unique artistic language, that were well-known among the whole world. Many poets of Song Dynasty by Ou Yangxiu, Mei Yaochen and other poems, are also related with purple sand tea sets. In 1976, villa calabash Hill unearthed a Song Dynasty ancient kiln ruins and early purple residue accumulation layer, found a pot and tank categories of pottery remains. Ming Jiajing to Wanli Years was mature period of Yixing purple. Previously, there were“Four Families” including Dong Han, Zhao Liang, Yuan Chang and Shi Peng. Then there were “Three Families” including Shi Dabin, Li Zhongfang and Xu Youquan. Beetle mud, enclosure, making cylinder forming method and clay pieces inlaid forming method gradually hasten to perfect. The late Ming Dynasty to the Qing Dynasty, as the purple sand crafts boom. Purple sand process to the decorative patterns, pattern shape development, appeared a lot of earthenware treasures with fine skills, perfect images and fiber dense structure. Modern and contemporary, Yixing purple sand reached its heyday. from the mud texture to process, from the purple research to school innovation were both developed, according to the relevant information documented in 1919, mountain residents in Shu shan, Ding shan, Tang du and chuan bu area, Yixing, “were all making pottery”. After the founding of the PRC, From the purple pot and flowerpot, purple sand production developed to hundreds varieties, many artists, skilled in pot art, painting and calligraphy, carving, flowerpot modeling and sculpture art grow with each passing day, not only products, but also the development of sculpture painting and ancient and modern character of sand sculpture works.

After a long history of ceramic artists’development, with integration of tea culture, as well as the ancient literati’highly praise and participation on purple sand pottery, Yixing purple sand has gone through 300 years of development, has created the inscriptions, mosaics (mosaic gold, silver, jade, color mud, mother-of-pearl, rosewood, porcelain flower), tinning, lacquer painting, mud painting, pastel, glaze, enamel, drawing, embossing, hollow carving, mud cutting, printing, sticking and a series of decorative crafts. Which the most representative is pottery carving, it is perfect combination of poetry, painting and calligraphy, seal cutting art and purple sand crafts. Conform to Chinese traditional aesthetic standards, especially identical with the aesthetic of literary class. Unparalleled beautiful sand soil and Reiki of Jiangnan landscape, cultivate a generation of artists, born in different poses of purple sand artwork, with its culture and high art, become common carrier of culture and art, Set up many mileposts for the Chinese traditional culture and world art and culture tour.

Purple sand teapot naturally known to the world, do you know Yixing has a tradition of baking purple wine bottle. Purple wine vessel has warm vessel, holding vessel and drinking vessel, etc., there are various shapes of the jug, glass. Nanjing Museum collect Xiang Shengsi peach-shaped purple cup, aggravation delicate, rosy color, that came from the Yixing kilns. Both dressed nectar wine, and dissemination of culture and history, which combines wine art, wine history, pottery art, ceramic art, painting, calligraphy, poetry, sculpture, folk customs as a whole, is a special kind of artwork. According to written records, Neolithic appeared pottery similar in shape to the later wine pottery and horns bronze drinking vessels of Shang Zhou period. In the Zhejiang Yuyao Hemudu Cultural Site in lower reaches of the Yangtze River, there have been excavated pottery wares closely related to drink wine behavior, some scholars judged to be China's first wine wares. Wine wares accounted for more than ninety percent of the unearthed pottery in Dafanzhuang ruins of Dawenkou Culture Site. The Neolithic to the Xia Dynasty, dominated by pottery drinking vessels, supplemented with copper and lacquer ware. Qin Han period, dominated by lacquer ware, supplemented with copper and jade wine vessels. Wei Jin period dominated by porcelain wine, supplemented with jade wine vessels. Tang Song to Ming Qing Dynasties, porcelain wine is still most popular. Plum-bottle was one of the wine vessels in Yuan Ming Qing era. From Wei Jin Dynasties to Tang Song Ming and Qing Dynasties, porcelain wine ware has captured the dominator. Ming and Qing Dynasties were prosperous time of China's ceramic industry development. During Ming Dynasty, in common with jade bottles, pear-shaped pot, dragon handle pot, plum-bottle, heart-shaped pot, celestial sphere-shaped pot, etc. In the decorative methods had Blue-and-white, underglaze red, white glaze, green glaze, red glaze, etc. Technology has painting, carving, hollowing, melon petal, stamping, bodiless, etc. The styling is richer, more varied varieties, such as reflux pot, warm pot.

The development course of Yixing ceramic drinking vessels, generally corresponding with wine history of our country. But also has its unique characteristics. First is Neolithic culture was long standing and well established, from the beginning, and after thousands of years, from the original red pottery, terracotta, celadon, and then to the purple sand crafts pottery, ceramics of modern celadon, Yixing ceramics had kept the torch aflame. Second is mainly civilian, wine products are mostly for people use in daily life, little tribute Royal for such exquisite masterpiece, and water ware, tea ware in contrast, autocratic, special usage is not very prominent. Third is the diversity of raw material, China clay, pottery clay, purple sand clay, have been widely used for firing pottery porcelain. In Yixing clay resources development and utilization in different historical periods, source of ore mining, clay refining technology constantly updated to improve, have extensive adaptability, practicability and diversity. even formulation of earthenware concept, is also insufficient for 1000 years. The fourth is due to local conditions, rich resources, clay flow field is insufficient, with local clay and mud as main raw materials; tea appreciation, porcelain trade convenient, with porcelain wine mainly. Firth is good at inheritance and innovation, porcelain and purple color, purple sand tire and glaze organic combination, all kinds of Purple ceramic bottle should appear, purple clay value and modern technological value show synchronously, promoting ceramic culture play profound movement.

Yixing purple sand ceramic bottle merged thick connotation of ceramic and the unique charm of Yixing purple culture, and culture of wine bottle, retroactive purple origin, refine ceramic character, comply with the trend, given the mission to the cultural heritage, technical innovation and economic prosperity, focused on the modes of production and life of people, common trait and culture aesthetic habits in the Yixing area, reflect the uniqueness, living state, inheritance, variability, integrity and regional features of intangible cultural heritage. These are the successful case of the productive protection, inheritance and innovation of intangible cultural heritage of traditional crafts. It can be said that the develop and expand of Chinese wine culture, make the traditional pottery culture open up a new exhibit stage, conversely, rich and colorful Chinese pottery culture, also promote the Chinese wine culture.

From the angle of baking pottery and porcelain, the main conditions of distinguishing pottery and porcelain are raw material and sintering temperature. With fine clay as blank, sintering temperature in the pottery desired level, for pottery, such as ancient white pottery. Fine clay in the china desired temperature, the blank will become china. Purple is a kind of special material between the porcelain and pottery, fine clay lithified to a certain extent began to crystallize into sand, then could be the purple sand. Fine clay fired at high temperature after its structure become crystal shape, internal structure is orderly closed, smooth surface, glassy, could be china. Lithified fine clay become sand crystal, the baked pottery scaly arranged internal. A chain of airway formed between the scales. The airway is minimal, water gain damping phenomenon under atmospheric pressure, then forming a permeable and impermeable purple. Both ventilation and porous ceramic is called pottery. In the thousands of years of ceramic baking, we could often see the purple, the ancients ceramic utensils material selection were not very accurate, but could just vary from general clay. During the Six Dynasties period, primitive celadon (glazed pottery) and products inputting green glaze, had appeared purple blank, the purple blank is not exactly the same as pottery blank usually seen. The color is closer to the purple sand blank of Ming Qing Dynasties from looking. This showed that purple and celadon in raw material utilization different approaches but equally satisfactory results, purple pottery produce techniques should be in certain aspects inherit achievements of celadon produce technology. In early Tang Dynasty, there had been a large number of celadon porcelain in Guijing, Yixing. Blank of porcelain then had already contains purple sand composition, showed that the ancients had already make use of purple sand raw materials either consciously or subconsciously.

With the progress of science and technology and the improvement of productivity in new technology and material innovation, raw materials in the pottery and porcelain have occupied a certain position. Purple ceramic bottle thus emerge as the times require. From material selection, grinding, selection of advanced modern technology and equipment and other aspects, applied method of “cracks” porcelain (surface cracks) to make wine bottle. That is namely adding transition layer between the glaze and blank, in order to offer different temperature for purple clay and glaze firing, so as to solve the technical problem of easily cracking in the condition of high temperature, eliminates the leakage defects that peculiar appearing in purple sand vessels, succeed to fulfill purple ceramic bottle finally, become new favorite among Yixing ceramics.

In the field of pottery baking crafts, Goldfish Purple Ceramic bottle realized organic union between purple mineral raw material and technology of ceramic properties; in the cultural inheritance aspect, it implemented organic combination with the traditional crafts, popular customs and local culture; in the management level, it realized organic combination with the cultural artwork and popular commodity, so that the traditional baking crafts of purple sand ceramic bottle, to raw materials and ceramic craft with strong, high-grade wine bottle and high-grade wine symbiosis, inheritance and innovation process condensate force strong characteristics, become upscale purple bottle innovation leader in this field. Become bright carrier that possess the purple culture image, ceramic technology characteristics and elegant consumption taste, forming distinct characteristics in the wine culture development.

Purple ceramic bottle of Goldfish Ceramics Limited Company have different poses and with different expressions, the figure is elegant, animal modeling are so skillfully imitated as to be indistinguishable from the original, lines concise, plant modeling seems true to life vividly. Its decorative culture is rich and colorful, there is a riot of colours in the glaze, enamel glaze with a non engobe unglazed and glazed color, rough handmade color, realistic image of reliefs, individual color blanks, simple natural sandblasting, even engraving that blending painting and calligraphy into one, luxuriant coating, and otherwise tailored crafts for wineries, decal decoration for trademarks and trademark describes, are unparalleled in the world. Ceramic wine bottle with its rich connotation and the appearance and texture have experienced years of wind and frost formation, most incisive display the broad and profound of wine culture, favored by the wine industries. over the years, goldfish ceramics has always maintained a strong sales in short supply, and become the industry leader, even made enormous contribution for dissemination of purple culture.

Publishing of the "Baking Crafts of Yixing Goldfish Purple Ceramic Wine Bottle" are also benefited from the experts' hard work from Shandong Intangible Cultural Heritage Research Center, Since August 2010, experts group stays in Yixing Dingshu Town, branching three dimensions including folk physical collection, behavior collection and information research, to carry on fieldwork. In the course of the investigation, to take baking crafts of Yixing goldfish purple ceramic wine bottle, representative inheritors and folk culture as the basic clue, summed up basic characteristics and core elements of baking crafts of Yixing goldfish purple ceramic wine bottle, and further analysis stable inheritance of baking crafts of Yixing goldfish purple ceramic bottle, and even in Dingshu Town, Yixing and Jiangsu-Zhejiang area, until drinking customs of the entire Chinese and contact between aesthetic psychology behind the cultural traits, spiritual beliefs and other demands, Seeking deep rules and forms of Yixing goldfish purple ceramic bottle baking crafts. Focus on systematic investigation and study on Yixing goldfish purple ceramic bottle and associated folk culture. Reveals the cultural significance and protective value of intangible cultural heritage in this productive process, Made positive efforts for the Yixing ceramic culture research, has achieved fruitful results. Here, as the promoter of Yixing ceramic culture, I wish to express our heartfelt thanks to friends from Shandong.

Shi Juntang

Vice-chairman of China Ceramics Industrial Association

November, 2011

中華民國五年六月測圖二十四年七月公路補正二十五年五月製版三十四年七月印刷
五萬分一之尺
軍事委員會軍令部

绪论

1 民国五年六月制宜兴地形图

一、宜兴金鱼紫砂陶瓷酒瓶烧造技艺研究背景

（一）所在区域辖属沿革

“失路荆溪上，依人忽暝投。长桥今夜月，阳羡古时州。野烧明山郭，寒更出县楼。先生能馆我，无事五湖游。”

——唐诗人严维《荆溪馆呈丘义兴》

宜兴历史悠久，文化鼎盛，其最早的人类居住历史可追溯至一万年前，据宜兴湖㳇镇灵谷洞的考古发掘证明，那个时期已经有古人类在这里活动。此后，在宜兴归径乡南唐村、骆驼墩，邮堂乡西溪村一带又先后发现了一批原始文化遗址，它们横跨新石器时代至商周时期，是当时宜兴人类文化发展的见证。之后大约在6000～7000年前，宜兴已进入了农业文明时代，并出现了原始的部落。

大约距今5000年左右宜兴进入了母系氏族阶段，这个时期的遗址代表为骆驼墩遗址，该遗址中出土了一系列的日用品，其中有不少的原始陶器，证明了至晚在这个时期，宜兴已开始了制陶历史。原始的农业在这个时期也有所发展，人们逐渐过上定居的生活，氏族成为人们活动的主要组织形式，女性在组织中占据着主导的地位。

随着农业的不断发展，男性的地位开始在组织中得到提升。直至距今约4000～5000多年前，父系氏族公社开始成为宜兴的主要社会组织，男性在社会中的地位首次得到展现。而此时的陶器制作技艺已有相当的发展，与骆驼墩遗址里的原始陶器相比，这一时期出土的陶器无论在形制还是烧制工艺上，都有了很大的改进，其中以宜兴杨巷、鼎蜀、张泽、铜峰、新芳、善卷一带出土的这一时期的器物最为典型。此时的村落已从原始的山林转移到靠近河边的高地和山麓南坡上，因为这样的地方最适宜开展农业生产，尤其是有着农业生产所必需的充足的水源和阳光。村落的规模也就母系氏族时期有所扩大，并逐渐出现大的村落联盟。此时期的工具仍以石器为主，不过已经开始出现原始的青铜使用迹象。

随着原始村落联盟的发展以及青铜在现实生产和生活中的运用，农业生产力得到了很大的提升，男耕女织的传统生活方式逐步出现。此时的织物仍以粗麻制品为主，人们在生活所需之外，有了一些生产的剩余，于

①骆驼墩遗址
②《宜兴县志》
③明万历十八年重修宜兴县志序
④宜兴太平天国王府
⑤国山碑院
⑥翟氏节孝坊

是交易开始在不同的村落之间出现，并随着青铜器的大规模使用及生产力的不断扩大，这种交易的范围不断扩大。为原始部落及部落联盟的出现奠定了基础。这与中国的大致历史发展进程基本相似。此后，经过漫长的发展，大致在新石器时期中晚期，宜兴进入了大型部落时代，青铜文明开始在这一时期的遗址中显示其重要分量。这一时期的陶器制作在实用的基础上，更加注重外观的打造和美化，烧制工艺上也就之前有很大提升，陶器的质量有了改观。

宜兴实现原始村落联盟向城镇的转变至晚在唐虞夏商时期就已完成，它成为周围不同村落和部落间交换东西的重要场所。手工业在这时已成为一个独立的产业开始发展，他们的主要活动区域就是人们交换东西的地方，前店后厂的传统“商铺+作坊”的雏形开始在这一时期出现。陶器制作也已成为一个独立的行当，农业生产之余，那些技术娴熟的陶匠们会聚集到一起烧制陶器，交流制陶心得，这促进了原始制陶技艺的改革和发展，为陶器实现质的飞跃提供了可能。

宜兴古称荆溪，归属扬州管辖，农业、手工业在其社会经济中起着重要的作用，城镇的发展已有所推进，原始的城镇形态中吴文化成为主流，这个时期的陶器制作就表现了鲜明的吴文化特色。大约在公元前473年，越王勾践经卧薪尝胆后，消灭了吴国，宜兴又成为越国的属地。这段历史开启了宜兴陶瓷发展的新纪元。据说，当年越王的得力助手范蠡助越王战胜吴国后，就挂印归隐，携西施一起来到了今日的宜兴。他们发现此地陶土甚多，且性能极佳，故而在此开窑烧陶，并开掘了“蠡河”以方便运输，一时间宜兴陶瓷名传全国，为世人所争抢。由此开启了宜兴烧陶的辉煌历史。公元前355年，越国又被楚国消灭，宜兴划归楚国管辖，这期间宜兴一直被称为 “荆邑”，吴越文化成为宜兴本地的主流文化，它们深深地影响着宜兴的社会生产和生活。此时期的很多陶器形制和装饰就体现了明显的吴越文化痕迹，至今许多优秀的形制就是从那一时期传下来的。

宜兴成为县府建城，完成于公元前221年。当时秦始皇统一全国后，推行郡县制。原来的楚国之地，被重新划分。宜兴由荆邑改为阳羡县，属新设置的会稽郡管辖，县城就位于现在的宜兴市区旧南门外土城新村。由此，拉开了宜兴的城市发展历史，陶器作为一个行业在这一时期也得到很大的发展。随着城市居民的出现，陶器也进入到独立的生产阶段，陶器制作工艺和烧制手法得到发展。

西汉时，汉高祖刘邦因灵常军功卓著，于公元前202年将此地封为灵常的封地，后于公元前168年重新收归政府，仍名为阳羡县，属会稽郡。汉光武帝（25）时将阳羡县改为阳羡邑，仍归会稽郡管辖。汉顺帝四年（129）会稽郡进行了重新划分，浙江东为会稽，西为吴郡（今苏州），宜兴仍称阳羡县，归属吴郡管辖。

三国时期，宜兴归属变革较大，范围也是时大时小，体现了这一时期的历史特点。吴黄武初年（222）时，宜兴被封为吴国第一任丞相孙邵的封国，其国都就位于现在江苏宜兴市的新街镇，之后收归国有，改为

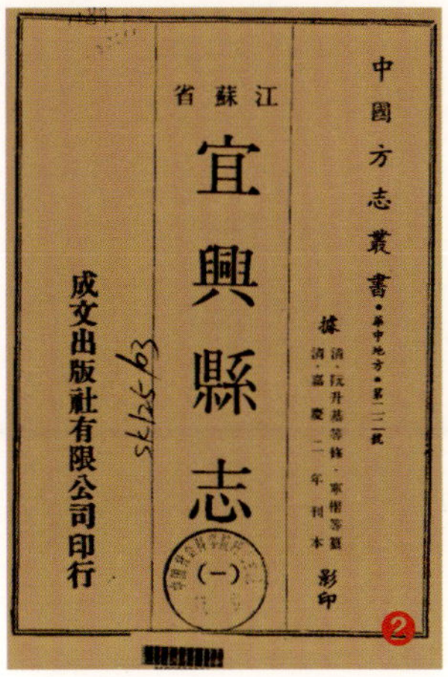

②

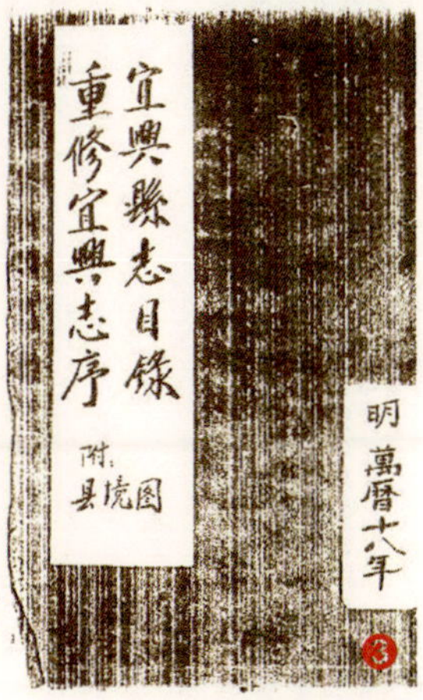

③

④

⑤

⑥

中华老字号

宜兴金鱼紫砂陶瓷酒瓶烧造技艺·研究背景

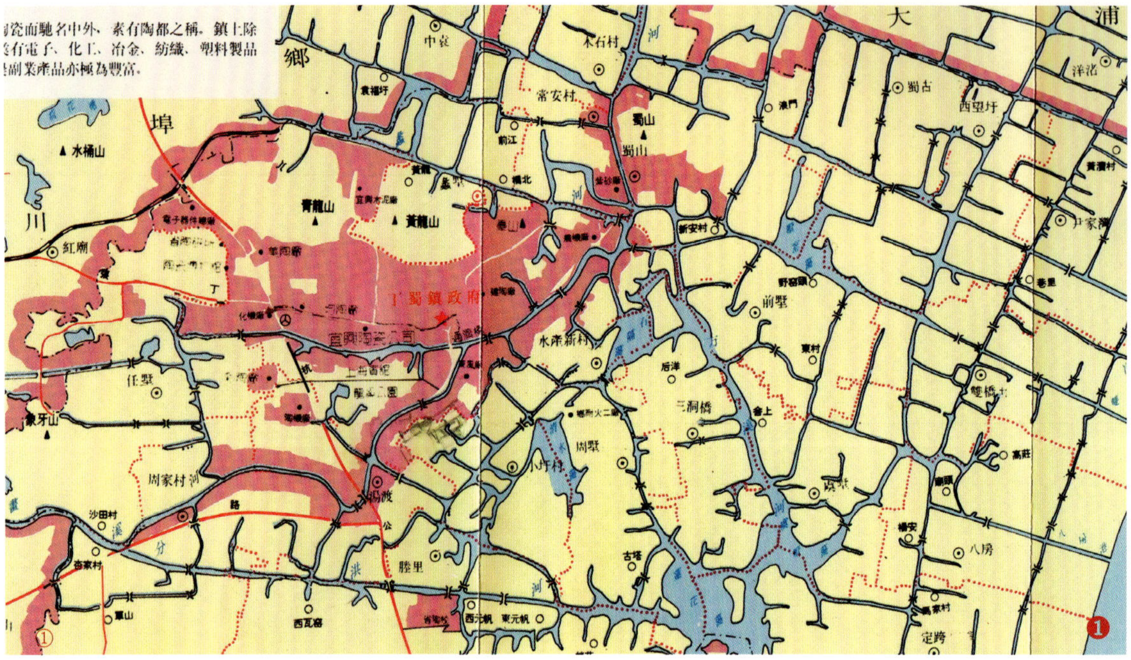

县，仍沿用阳羡之名。吴宝鼎元年（266），吴帝孙皓设置吴兴郡（今湖州），阳羡县就划归吴兴郡管辖，面积较之前有所变化。晋灭吴后，晋惠帝永兴元年（304），惠帝司马衷将阳羡、国山、临津（三地均属原阳羡县）、永世、平陵（此两地在今丹阳南部、溧阳境）、义乡（现长兴县）六县设为义兴郡，以表彰江南士族首脑周处长子周玘“三定江南”义兵之功。

南北朝时，宜兴的面积减小，归属再次发生变化。宋武帝永初三年（422）时，分割阳羡义乡、宣城郡的广德、吴兴郡的故鄣、长城五县境内相临近的地域设置绥安县，管辖者仍为义兴郡。文帝嘉元九年（432），平陵县被并入溧阳，永世县归入丹阳，宜兴的归属此时期没有太大变化，区域上也变动不大。明帝泰始四年（468），义兴郡被划归南徐州（今镇江）管辖，其下辖的几个县也同时划归南徐州。齐武帝永明二年（484），义兴郡又划为扬州管辖，之后再次归属南徐州。

隋朝时，宜兴阳羡之名被废，改为义兴县，其原有境域不变，同时并入义乡、国山、临津三县，归常州府管辖。宜兴陶瓷此时在全国已具有相当的名气，很多皇家的御用瓷器就出自这里。

唐武德二年（619），义兴县改为鹅州，分置阳羡、临津两县，国山县被废；唐武德七年（624），鹅州被改为南兴州，分置临津、义兴、阳羡三县；唐武德八年（625）南兴州又被废，临津、阳羡二县也同时废除，只保留义兴县，归常州府管辖。唐肃宗乾元二年（759），义兴县改归润州（今镇江）管辖，次年（760）又重新归属常州府。变化之频繁，堪称历史之最。

由“义兴县”改为“宜兴县”完成于宋太宗太平兴国元年（976），原是为避赵光义之名讳而更改，这也是“宜兴”一词第一次出现在历史典籍当中。此后，终宋一朝，未曾有所更改，宜兴的经济也与此时进入快速的发展当中。

元朝时，宜兴再次进入归属名称频繁变化时期。元世祖至元十二年（1275），宜兴县改为南兴军；十四年（1277）改回宜兴县，属常州路管制；十五年（1278）宜兴县提升为宜兴府，管辖区域扩大；二十年（1283）又降为宜兴县，仍属常州路；二十一年（1284）再次升为宜兴府，置宜兴县发隶之。元成宗元贞元年（1295），府县俱废，改设宜兴州，仍隶属常州路。元惠宗至正十六年（1356），张士诚派唐本初据守，十八年（1358）归附。

经历了元朝的不断变更，宜兴境域也有很大变化，不过基本的框架仍然保留，陶瓷业在宜兴的经济中始终占据着重要的位置，成为当地民众重要的经济来源之一。明朝建立初期，保留了元朝宜兴州的建制。明洪武元年（一说二年）（1368）时，宜兴州改为宜兴县，属常州府管辖，直隶京师。此建制一直延续至清朝。清雍正四年（1726）时，宜兴县被拆分为宜兴、荆溪二县，都由常州府管辖。

①丁蜀镇行政区图
②城隍庙戏楼
③清重建岳忠武王宗祠残碑
④丁蜀镇老街
⑤中国宜兴陶瓷博物馆

后约二百年未曾变化，直至1911年11月6日。随着中国民主革命的兴起和高涨，宜兴县成立了军政府，正式脱离清朝的管制。民国元年荆溪县撤销，并入宜兴县，在1914—1927年期间属苏常道管制。抗战期间，由中国共产党领导的人民政权在宜兴南部山区设立宜溧县，在太湖沿岸一带建立武宜县，宜兴进入了动荡的战乱时期。这一时期宜兴的陶瓷生产基本上处于停滞状态，没有技术上的革新和突破。

1949年4月24日，宜兴获得解放。同年5月2日，宜兴县成立了军事管制委员会，不久又成立了中共宜兴县委和宜兴县人民政府，6月改属常州专区管辖。1952年划归江苏省苏州专区；1953年1月26日属苏州专区；1956年2月17日属镇江专区；1958年8月镇江专区机关迁至常州市，改称常州专区；1959年9月专区机关迁回镇江市，仍称镇江专区；1967年3月改称镇江地区；1983年1月18日起，属无锡市；1983年3月正式划归无锡市；1988年1月撤销宜兴县，设宜兴市（县级市）。

2000年“撤乡并镇”期间，宜兴市内的乡镇作了较大调整，原有的红塔镇并入宜城镇；原有的善卷镇并入张渚镇；原有的西渚、元上两乡合并为西渚镇；原有的宜丰镇、潘家坝乡并入徐舍镇；原有的堰头乡并入鲸塘镇；原有的钮家乡、都山乡并入官林镇；原有的南新镇并入和桥镇；原有的南漕镇并入万石镇；原有的分水镇并入周铁镇；原有的扶风镇并入芳桥镇；原有的大塍镇并入新庄镇；原有的张泽镇并入大浦镇；原有的归径乡并入新街镇……经调整后的宜兴市下辖28个镇，共有人口约106万余人。

2004年宜兴行政区划再次作出调整，下属乡镇除宜兴环保科技工业园区外，官林镇与丰义镇合并组建新的官林镇，张渚镇与茗岭镇合并组建新的张渚镇，和桥镇与闸口镇合并组建新的和桥镇，丁蜀镇与洑东镇合并组建新的丁蜀镇，周铁镇与洋溪镇合并组建新的周铁镇，杨巷镇与新芳镇合并组建新的杨巷镇，高塍镇与范道镇合并组建新的高塍镇，市辖乡镇数量由之前的28个调整为21个，减小了冗余环节，提升了市内的行政效率。

2007年4月2日，根据《无锡市人民政府关于调整宜兴市部分行政区划的批复》及《省政府关于同意调整宜兴市部分行政区划的批复》（苏政复[2007]23号）精神，宜兴市内行政区划再次作出调整：原宜兴市鲸塘镇、芳庄镇与徐舍镇合并设立新的徐舍镇，镇政府驻徐舍；撤销宜兴市大浦镇，将原大浦镇管辖的张泽、大浦2个居委会和双庙、施

2

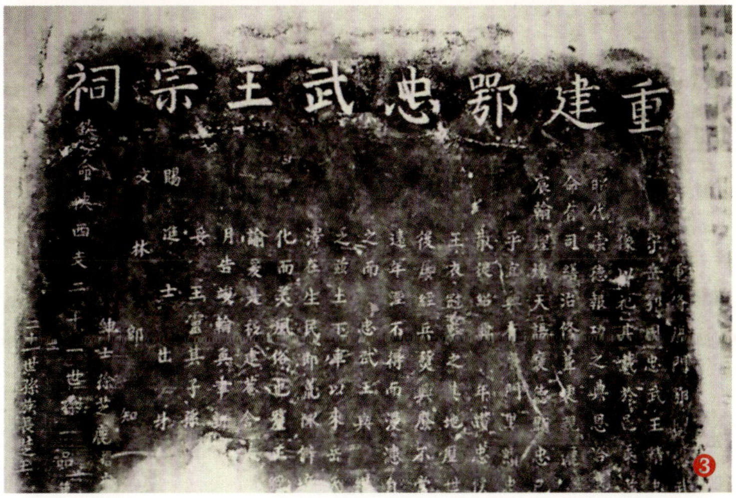

3

4

5

荡、北塘、张泽、毛旗、方钱、大浦、浦南、汤庄、渭渎、洋渚、洋岸12个村委会划归丁蜀镇管辖；撤销宜兴市新街镇，将其原辖区域与宜城街道办事处管理的绿园、文昌2个居委会和南河、铜峰、南岳、梅园、谢桥5个村委会合并设立新街街道办事处；将宜兴市原大浦镇管辖的山林、南园2个村委会划归宜城街道办事处管理；将宜城街道办事处的花圩、东梅、杏里、文庄、轸村、东郊、边庄7个村委会划归屺亭街道办事处管理；将宜城街道办事处的红塔、肖庄、宋渎、徐家桥、桂庄5个村委会划归高塍镇管辖；撤销宜兴市新庄镇，以其原辖区域设立新庄街道办事处。调整之后，宜兴由19个镇调整为14个，再一次提升了行政办公效率，降低了当地的财政负担，加快了当地经济的发展。

金鱼陶瓷所在的丁蜀镇位于宜兴市东南部，东濒太湖，南靠浙江省长兴县，西邻湖汶镇，北接宜城镇、大浦镇，是宜兴市陶瓷发展较为先进的一个城镇。全镇总面积约有97.75平方千米，常住人口约12.788万。镇人民政府驻东坡路，位于市政府驻地东南约10千米处。

该镇1956年成立，由丁山、蜀山、汤渡三地合并而成，取前二者首字得名。1959年1月改为丁蜀公社，1959年5月，仍改为丁蜀镇，1986年周墅乡并入该镇，1992年川埠乡并入，2004年洑东镇并入。至2005年时，丁蜀镇全镇共下辖有定溪、双桥、尹家、西望、蜀山、通蜀、芳溪、三洞桥、周墅、塍里、建新、任墅、红卫、赵庄、蒋笠、上坝、凰川、前龙、大港、兰山、洑东、陶淋、川埠、查林、洛涧、潜洛、头阳、紫砂28个村和蜀北、航运、南河、蠡墅、湖渎、丁山、解放、西庄、东山前、化新、张边、鑫圩、丁南、公园路、彩陶、南山、龙溪、画溪、汤渡、潘南20个社区（其中，川埠、查林、洛涧、潜洛、头阳、紫砂6个村实际由环科园管理）。2006年，宜兴市委、市政府又将川埠村、查林村、洛涧村、潜洛村、头阳村、紫砂村6个行政村成建制划归丁蜀镇管理，扩大了丁蜀镇的管理权限。现在该镇已成为宜兴市数一数二的陶瓷生产重镇，在金鱼等知名陶瓷企业的带领下，不断创造出一个又一个陶瓷奇迹。

（二）所在区域地理环境

“位置优越，物产丰饶，乃江南佳处，不可多得。”

宜兴市位于江苏省西南端、沪宁杭经济三角的中心地带，东面太湖与苏州相连，南接浙江长兴县，西南临安徽广德县，西濒溧阳县，西北与金坛相连，北部又与武进相依，是一个自然与人文汇聚的佳地。这里得天独厚的自然条件和丰富的瓷土和紫砂泥矿藏，为陶瓷业的发展提供了方便，因而历来是陶瓷业的龙头所在，尤其是紫砂和青瓷业的发展，更是为全国之翘楚，我们著名的金鱼陶瓷就是诞生在这样一个地方。

宜兴总面积约有2038.7平方千米，其中太湖水面就有约208.7平方千米。境内水域面积辽阔，大小湖泊镶嵌其间，西氿、团氿、东氿三氿相伴于市区两侧。这里的城市化率已高达60%，就是乡村也已基本实现现代化，是我国少有的几个经济全面发展的县级市之一。

市内的地势呈现出南高北低走势，其西南部为连绵起伏的低山丘陵地带，北部为一马平川的平原区域，东部为广阔的太湖水域，西部则为低洼的圩区，与水有关的区域占了这里不小的一块儿，为当地的工农业生产用水及发展提供了方便。目前全市共有耕地面积约6.49万公顷、山林面积约4.88万公顷、水域面积约294.3平方千米，水库塘河总容量可达1.31亿立方米，常年可利用水资源有10.67亿立方米，基本上可满足宜兴的生活和生产用水需求。

宜兴还是一个矿产资源十分丰富的地区，其现已探明的矿种有27种之多，包括石灰岩、大理岩、太湖石、石英砂岩、煤、泥炭等，瓷土及紫砂矿是其中最具开发价值的矿产之一，尤其蜀山独有的陶土更是制作紫砂器具的上等原料。这里的非金属矿主要有黏土矿，矿种有甲泥、紫砂泥、白泥、嫩泥、绿泥、黑泥、小红泥、小黄泥等等，现已探明工业储量约6000万吨，预测远景储量在10亿吨左右：其中瓷石瓷土矿储量在200万吨以上；烧制水泥和石灰的优质原料石灰石，预计储量约17亿吨左右；宜兴的大理石有红奶油、咖啡和黑色等稀有种类，估计储量约5000万立方米；而建筑石储量达百亿吨；此外还有大量烧制玻璃用的石英砂及白云石、型砂、重晶石等。另外，宜兴境内地下还储有可燃有机矿如煤矿、泥炭等，其中煤矿的探明储量约4600万吨，这

①沈氏旧居砖墙

些储量丰富的煤矿为陶瓷烧制提供了丰富的燃料。

宜兴全年温暖湿润，太阳光照充足，热量条件较好，年平均气温为15.7℃，夏季最热月平均气温为28.3℃。年平均无霜期为240余天，可供作物利用的生长期达250天左右，非常适合各种植物生长和繁育。这里的农作物一般为一年2～3熟，水稻在其种植面积中占有重要的比例。区域内降水十分丰沛，全年都有雨水，年平均雨日约为136.6天，平均每三天就有一天下雨，年平均降水量可达1177毫米，其中尤以春夏雨水最为集中，这为各种作物的生长雨水提供了丰富的供给。

宜兴地形复杂，土壤种类众多。据1959年的土壤普查结果显示，宜兴拥有约113.73万亩耕地，可分为11类，30个土种。其中水田面积约105.04万亩，平原圩区的土壤有乌泥土类、黄泥土类、沙泥土类、白土类等；丘陵冲田的土壤分乌泥土类、黄土类、冲田白土、沙泥类等等；宜兴旱地面积约8.7万亩，其中沿太湖渎区土壤分有夜潮土类、山黄泥土类、山白土类、沙土类等。1979—1982年的土壤普查，更是将其土壤精确地分为7个土类、13个亚类、31个土属。丰富的土壤种类和复杂的地形，为这里多样化的种植业发展提供了良好的自然条件，除水稻、蔬菜等农作物的生产外，这里还是著名的茶乡竹海，江苏最大的产茶基地、连片面积最大的竹海就位于其境内。这里广阔的山地中，还种植着面积不少的杉木、马尾松、檫木、樟树、紫楠、红楠、麻栎、榆树、榉树等多种优良用材树种，为陶瓷业及工农业生产用林提供了保证。

位于宜兴城西南部茗岭乡境内的龙池山就是当地著名的森林自然保护区。其海拔为488米，森林覆盖率达95%。这里属于中亚热带北缘，常绿宽叶林在此处生长茂盛，除上面提到的一些树种外，如金钱松、天目玉兰等珍贵树种也生长在这里，是我国著名的植物种子资源库，故有“天然植物王国”和“绿色氧吧”之称。

优越的自然条件也为各种动物的生长繁衍提供了便利，这里生活着野鸡、黄雀、黄鹂、画眉等上百种鸟类，银鱼、鳜鱼、黄鳝、青鱼、草鱼、鲢鱼等数十种鱼类，猎狗、狼、野猪、狐、刺猬、松鼠、穿山甲、野兔等各类珍稀野生哺乳动物，是江南动物资源的重要汇集地。

凭借着这些天然的自然条件和丰富的物产，加上宜兴人辛勤的耕耘和付出，这里成为了陶文化、茶文化、竹文化和洞穴文化繁荣的著名地区。2009年，宜兴市在全国县域经济基本竞争力排名中首次跃居第六位，成为中国数一数二的经济大县，现在正向着经济强县的目标迈进。而这些离不开其陶瓷业的发展和助力。

（三）所在区域经济环境

“陶的古都，瓷的世界，纺织、制茶的天堂……”

①

②

金鱼陶瓷所在的宜兴市位于沪、宁、杭经济三角的中心地带，处于苏、浙、皖三省的交界区，历来就是交通便捷，商贾云集，经济发达的工商业重镇。全市现设14个镇、4个街道、1个国家级高新技术开发区、2个省级经济开发区，是我国县域经济快速发展的典型代表和地区。

得益于这里优越的自然地理优势，宜兴的国民经济发展实现了平衡快速增长。2009年全年，全市地区生产总值达680.68亿元，比上年同期增长11.7%。人均地区生产总值为5.38万元，远远高于全国同类县市的平均值。第一、二、三产业的增加值分别为32.14亿元、382.39亿元、266.15亿元，其中第三产业的增值加快，高附加值产业在其中占了很大的比例。2009年宜兴财政总收入达103.88亿元，比上年同期增长18.05%，其中一般预算性收入为45.02亿元，超过同类县市的平均值；财政总支出约70亿元，其中一般性预算支出约48.69亿元，

①宜兴茶园
②宜兴竹海
③小窑墩遗址（西晋）
④江家桥
⑤团氿风景区
⑥三官堂遗址
⑦下湾遗址

远低于同类县市的平均值。一边是高度发展的工商业生产收入，一边是不断降低的财政支出，这使得宜兴在2009年末被评为全国县域经济基本竞争力第六位。

在宜兴人民共同的努力下，宜兴现已形成了以环保设备、电线电缆、精细化工、陶瓷、冶金、化纤织造、服装服饰为主的产业集群，以及包括机电、轻工、新材料、新能源等行业门类齐全、布局合理、协作配套能力较强的工业体系，培育了金鱼陶瓷、鹏鹞环保、远东线缆、灵谷尿素、虎皇油漆、银鱼餐具等一批在国内外具有较强竞争力的名牌产品，为全市经济的后续发展提供了助力和保障。

陶瓷产业：宜兴被誉为“陶的古都”，早在7000多年前，宜兴就已开始了早期的制陶历史。这里的陶瓷制作集保健实用、艺术鉴赏于一体，尤以紫砂茶具闻名海内外，其所做紫砂媲美均陶、精陶、青瓷、彩陶等，巧夺天工，堪称典范。在浓厚的陶瓷文化熏陶下，宜兴的陶瓷业得到了迅猛的发展。目前，宜兴拥有各类陶瓷企业近千家，2005年仅陶瓷业一项就实现了工业销售收入60亿元，其产品涉及日用陶瓷、建筑陶瓷、艺术陶瓷、工业陶瓷及紫砂陶瓷五大类2000多种产品，其中无铅釉下彩餐具、耐磨耐腐的工业陶瓷、美术陶瓷、纳米陶瓷材料、陶瓷机械、紫砂工艺品等更是在国内外陶瓷市场上占有较高份额。金鱼陶瓷的系列酒瓶产品也在国内市场中占据主导地位，尤其是其生产的紫砂酒瓶，填补了国内紫砂酒瓶的空白，成为国内首家制成和成批生产紫砂酒瓶的知名企业。

茶叶生产：宜兴四季分明，阳光充足，雨水较多，且分布有连片的丘陵山地，这为茶叶的生产提供了条件，宜兴“阳羡雪芽”更是获得国家地理标志保护，成为远近闻名的知名茶品牌。宜兴也被誉为“茶的绿洲”。

竹子生产：宜兴优越的气候条件及成片的山区，为这里的竹子生产提供了便利。目前宜兴毛竹生长纵横八百余里，连绵几十万亩。仅“宜兴竹海风景区”中心面积就有一万亩，因而获得“华东第一竹海”、“太湖第一源”、“苏南第一峰”的美称。

环保机械产业：宜兴是我国重要的环保机械产业基地，其环保机械的生产和研发能力在全国同类县市中名列前茅。目前，全市共有环保企业1000余家，其中拥有全国百强环保企业14家，江苏省百强环保企业40家，成为全国县级市中单位面积内环保企业最多的地方。2005年一年仅环保企业一项实现工业销售收入83亿元，为其国民经济发展的重要构成。目前，宜兴市的各类环保企业已形成以水处理设备为主，包括声、气、固、仪、配件六大类200多个系列2000多个环保产品在内的生产能力，并形成集研发、设计、制造、工程、服务于一体的环保工业体系。在环保日益受到社会各界关注的今天，它们的发展潜力不可限量。

电线电缆产业：宜兴市主要的经济支柱产业之一，改革开放以来，宜兴电线电缆产业就异军突起，迅猛发展，成为全国数一数二的电线电缆产业基地。目前全市共拥有各类生产企业418家，其拥有量居全国同类县市前列，生产总量占到全国的15%强。这些企业中国家级高新技术企业

为5家，省级高新技术企业为9家，国家免检企业为3家。所生产的产品中有6个为中国驰名商标，3个为国家免检产品，1个为中国名牌产品，15个为省级名牌产品，25个为无锡市名牌产品。这些电线电缆有效地支撑了宜兴经济的发展，仅2005年一年就实现工业销售收入132亿元，成为宜兴经济的重要支柱。现在，宜兴出产的电线电缆产品主要涉及电力电缆、通信电缆、电气装备用电线电缆等，同时拥有了一大批与之相配套的铜材、电缆料加工企业，现已构成一个完整的产业链，助力着宜兴经济的发展与腾飞。

精细化工产业：精细化工在宜兴的产业格局中有着重要的分量，是宜兴GDP的重要贡献者。目前，宜兴拥有各类精细化工企业650余家，仅2005年一年就实现工业销售收入145亿元，为市内经济发展提供了充足的经济支持。宜兴出产的各类精细化工产品涉及化工领域11大类上千个品种，其中很多特色产品已经在国内国际上具有相当的知名度，如印染助剂、橡塑助剂、表面活性剂、纺织助剂、皮面助剂、水处理药剂等特色助剂现已成为全国知名产品。其中橡塑发泡剂、塑料抗氧剂、纺丝油剂、醇胺系列、环氧树脂等的生产技艺，更是领先于全国其他同类企业，成为国内技术领先产品，其生产的产品供不应求，极大地带动了当地经济的发展。而醇酸树脂、丙乙烯树脂、呋喃树脂、脲醛树脂等合成树脂的产量和质量也均在全国名列第一，影响和左右着国内的同类产品供应。民用油漆涂料生产也是其中很大的一块，其年产量超过10万吨，占到全国总产量的8%，为国内知名的“油漆之乡”。

纺织服装产业：宜兴的传统产业之一，与陶瓷业一样有着悠久的历史和传承，也是当地重要的经济支持产业之一，其出产的纺织服装在全国享有很高的声誉。目前，宜兴市拥有各类纺织企业932家，2005年一年就为宜兴市贡献工业销售收入101亿元，有效的支撑了当地的经济发展。经过多年的技术改革和创新，目前宜兴的纺织服装行业已形成集化纤、棉纺织、毛纺织、亚麻纺织、丝绸、色织、针织、印染、后整理、服装、非织造织物、纺机等门类为一体的产业体系，极大地提升了区域竞争力和发展力，为宜兴经济未来的发展提供了保障和助力。

冶金产业：尽管宜兴的金属矿产十分有限，但这并不能影响宜兴在这方面的发展和进步。经过改革开放以来多年的摸索和发展，宜兴冶金行业已进入高速发展的时期。目前，全市拥有各类冶金企业980余家，2005年一年完成工业销售收入175亿元，成为宜兴经济发展的重要支撑。宜兴的冶金产业现已形成集钢铁、有色、耐火、稀土四大板块为一体的冶金工业体系，并继续朝着高、精、尖的方向发展，预计未来发展前途无限。

旅游产业：工商业的发展，为宜兴旅游业的发展提供了经济基础和保障。宜兴现已形成以善卷洞风景区、竹海风景区、龙背山森林公园、宜园、陶祖圣境风景区5个国家AAAA级风景区为核心、近20个独立景点为补充、四通八达的旅游干线相连接的全新旅游版图，旅游接待和开发能力全面提升。仅2009年一年，全市旅游接待人数实现850万人次，创下历史新高。围绕旅游的发展，宜兴更是提出“中国陶都、生态宜兴”的城市定位，以加快实施“旅游振兴”战略。截至目前，宜兴市已获得“中国优秀旅游城市”、“国家园林城市”、“国家卫生城市”、“国家环境保护模范城市”、“全国生态示范区”、“中国民间梁山伯祝英台之乡” 等

①东坡书院
②归径桥
③苏东坡楚颂贴碑
④文昌阁

荣誉，成为吸引游客的重要卖点。

截至2010年年底，宜兴全市实现GDP收入807亿；工业总产值约2300.17亿元，规模以上工业产值1973.33亿；财政收入151.06亿，一般预算58.02亿；社会消费品零售总额274.81亿；进出口总额42.4856亿美元，出口26.4906亿美元。全社会固定资产投资完成额为359.73亿元，位居全国同类县市前列。其经济发展成果主要表现在以下几个方面：

经济综合实力大幅攀升。宜兴市地区生产总值突破500亿元大关，一般预算收入跃上30亿元新台阶。人均地区生产总值超6400美元，年均递增21.2%。财政总收入、一般预算收入分别相当于2002年的3.3倍和3.7倍。经济综合实力继续位居全国百强县（市）前列。

全面小康社会如期建成。城镇居民人均可支配收入、农民人均纯收入分别年均递增15.1%和12%，城乡居民人均储蓄存款2.5万元，家庭轿车拥有量超3.8万辆，城市和农村人均住房面积分别比2002年增加3.4和5.4平方米，“五保合一”的社会保障体系更加健全，为构建高水平全面小康，向率先基本实现现代化迈进奠定了坚实基础。

山水园林城市初步建立。团氿风景区、龙背山森林公园等一批市政重点工程顺利完成，城市“东进序曲”全面开启，城市建成区面积扩大到59.6平方公里，城市化水平提高到57%。先后被命名为国家园林城市、国家卫生城市、国家环境保护模范城市和全国生态示范区。

大交通格局基本形成。五年中用于交通建设的资金达37.8亿元，是前五年的3.3倍。新、改建公路93.5公里、桥梁650座，全社会通车总里程达到2200公里，比2002年增加了400公里。“两高一铁”先后贯通，104国道、342省道等国省干线和芜申运河、锡溧漕河全面改造提升，交通建设实现历史性跨越。

体制机制效应逐步显现。致力用改革的思路突破体制上的束缚，行政区划、企事业单位、财政、投融资、机构、农村等重点改革取得重要成果。致力扩大对外开放，累计到账外资14亿美元，完成进出口总额45亿美元，今年的到账外资和进出口总额分别是2002年的4倍和5.3倍；企业境外上市“宜兴板块”初步形成，经济国际化进程明显加快。

目前，宜兴整体经济社会保持着又好又快的发展，各项事业继续蓬勃向前，市政府正致力打造转型发展最快、功能布局最优、城市品质最佳、城乡一体化水平最高、环境优化增长最领先、人民群众幸福感最强的现代化城市，力求让宜兴成为“最适合人居、环境最好、发展最协调的地方”。

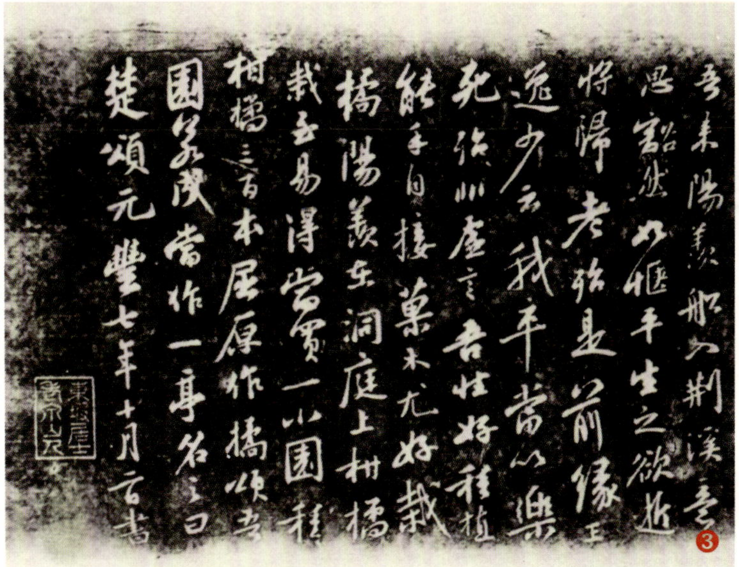

中华老字号

宜兴金鱼紫砂陶瓷酒瓶烧造技艺·研究方法

二、宜兴金鱼紫砂陶瓷酒瓶烧造技艺研究方法

"严谨的研究，是为了更好的继承和发展！"

田野工作（fieldwork，又可译为田野调查、现场调查、实地调查），是一种在各个学科里广泛应用的方法。历史考古学、民俗学、地质学、生物学、医学等等都在使用这一方法。从本课题的研究对象角度来看，宜兴金鱼紫砂陶瓷酒瓶烧造技艺是传统手工技艺的一个重要门类，因而它与其他传统手工技艺一样具有审美的本质，这是必须首先确定的。但是老字号中的传统手工制作技艺又有别于其他民间传统手工技艺，有它自己的特质，包含着丰富的文化内涵，这就要求研究方法、手段必须是多样的。民族学、民俗学、历史学、宗教学、考古学、社会学、以至于理学等诸多学科的理论方法在传统手工技艺研究中是经常被采用的。

本课题以田野专题调查的方法，将于2010年8月起，在江苏宜兴紫砂陶瓷传统制作技艺产地进行先期的田野调查。准备在此背景上，重点选取"金鱼紫砂陶瓷老字号"作为个案，进行系统和深入的田野考察。

非物质文化遗产不同于物质文化遗产，这是一种活态的文化，大多由传承人言传身授、代代沿承，以"活态"的形式流传扩散，历年历代生生不息。非物质文化遗产受制于内外有别、秘而不宣等家族式生产的师训旧规，有些还要依赖特定的传承人解读、释疑、获取，所以非物质文化遗产的研究、记录因其"活性"特点而难于保护、介绍，更难于广泛的流传，随经济的发展及文化的开放，现代的研究、记录及保存过程中采用了一些先进的手段，将非物质遗产物化为物质载体。记录和保存记录是最为基本和重要的工作，使传承人的活动方式、传承手段、传承条件、传承内容和传承结果物质形态化并进行有效保存。

非物质文化遗产的创造主体是广大的人民群众，中华大地的田间地头、村巷作坊是其生成流传的大舞台，是非物质文化遗产孕育、承传的主要场所。哪里有人群生息和劳作，哪里就有民间文化的创造和传播，民间的非物质文化具有历史、地理、民俗、宗教、人文、社会、心理、经济、政治等广泛而具体的内涵和价值，是国情、民族、民情的重要组成，也是有独特载体的民众的文化，涵盖了所有阶层文化中非物质形态的部分。对于非物质文化遗产的研究保护，需要广泛搜集各种类型的载体资源，既包括与之相关的文献资料，还包括相关交叉学科、基础学科的信息记载，要全方位、多层次的记录、研究，才能揭示某项非物质文化遗产的表象及真实内涵。

宜兴金鱼紫砂陶瓷酒瓶烧造技艺属传统工艺的范畴，它同样诞生于中华大地的民间沃土，发扬光大在宜兴乡间，因此田野调查是记录、研究其工艺的重要手段。田野调查在西方最早应用，英文名field work，这是一系列活动过程的概括，其含义是经过专门训练的人类学调查员亲自深入民间，以直接观察、访谈、住居体验为主要参与方式，从中获取第一手研究资料。它是人类学的核心内容，是一种实地获得文化理解的方

①

①田野考察专家组在前墅龙窑调研
②④⑤宜兴金鱼紫砂陶瓷酒瓶烧造技艺研讨会现场
③⑥⑦⑧⑨⑩⑪田野考察专家组工作现场

老字号文化遗产研究重点科研项目
宜兴金鱼紫砂陶瓷酒瓶烧造技艺学术研讨会

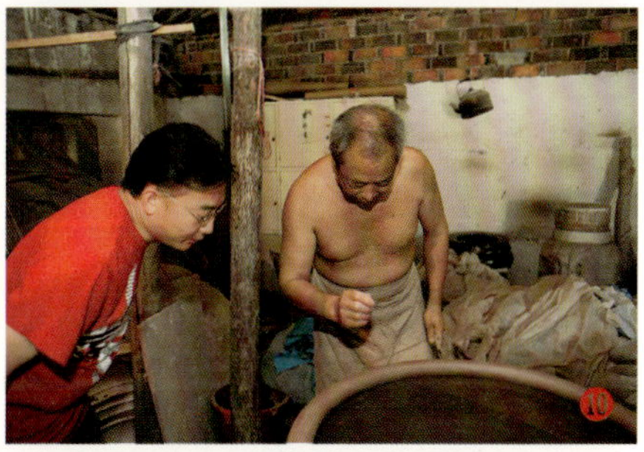

法及其研究技术与工具的手段，也是文化实践的认识论和方法论。我们的田野调查尚未彻底做到人类学意义上的田野调查的高度，限于人力物力等方面原因的限制，我们截取了田野调查的部分过程，以采风、访谈及采集资料等方式进行调查研究。通过受调查人的配合，我们带回诸多的文字资料、影像资料及实物资料等等，回到驻地，再加以分析综合。

对宜兴金鱼紫砂陶瓷酒瓶烧造技艺的田野专题调查自2010年8月开始，在宜兴市丁蜀镇进行了先期采访调查。在调查过程中，我们以宜兴金鱼紫砂陶瓷酒瓶烧造技艺、代表传承人、民俗文化等方面的田野考察为基本线索，归纳出宜兴金鱼紫砂陶瓷酒瓶烧造技艺的基本特征和核心元素，并进一步分析作为宜兴金鱼紫砂陶瓷酒瓶烧造技艺的稳定传承，及其在丁蜀镇、宜兴甚至江浙一带，直到整个中国的饮酒习俗和审美心理背后的文化特质、精神信仰等需求之间的联系，探求宜兴金鱼紫砂陶瓷酒瓶烧造技艺的深层方式和基本规律。我们不仅是调查了宜兴金鱼紫砂陶瓷酒瓶的制作、销售、品牌及市场知名度，更将其背后所深藏的历史、生活、民俗和活的传承人作为宝贵的非物质文化遗产来加以记录、研究和评述。因此，本课题重点对宜兴金鱼紫砂陶瓷酒瓶和与之相关的民俗文化进行系统的考察与整理研究，深入挖掘了这独特紫砂陶瓷酒瓶制作工艺所具有的重要的文化意义和非物质文化遗产的保护价值，对宜兴紫砂陶瓷酒瓶老字号文化遗产的多元文化传播和本土文化精神的树立有着时代的发展意义和广泛的现实意义。

对于宜兴金鱼紫砂陶瓷酒瓶烧造技艺的研究整理工作主要采取田野考察和历时性研究加逻辑分析等方法，非物质文化可分为物质、行为、精神意识三个层面，我们对宜兴金鱼紫砂陶瓷酒瓶烧造技艺的田野调查也分为三个层次：民俗实物征集、行为采录和资料研究，在这些工作的基础上，我们对得到的资料及信息反馈，结合理论进行了逻辑分析，力求将宜兴金鱼紫砂陶瓷酒瓶烧造技艺全方位、多角度的记录下来，并挖掘出其更深层次的文化价值，协助其继续发扬光大。

民俗实物征集。在陶都宜兴发达的陶瓷工业的影响下，宜兴金鱼紫砂陶瓷酒瓶烧造技艺的传承扎实而富有创新精神的从容沿承。在传承人的帮助下，我们收集到不少紫砂及陶瓷酒瓶制作先人曾使用过的工具、器物，也见识了很多先进的制瓶器具和紫砂制作工具，目睹了金鱼陶瓷开创以来的珍贵作品及现代的杰出产品等等。这些实物各具特色，其不同时代的作品记录了金鱼陶瓷的发展沿承历史，每个年代都有着明显的时代印记，展现了不同的技艺水平，五花八门的制瓷制瓶工具各有其独特的功用和使用方法，几乎每件或新或旧的器物上都有一段生动的故事。

行为采录。工艺的传承必然要人的参与，人是工艺的载体，工艺的传承人对行业的发展有着至关重要的作用。金鱼草陶的传承人自然是我们研究工作的重中之重。与其他手工工艺不同的是，宜兴金鱼紫砂陶瓷酒瓶烧造技艺是在一个开放的环境中于师徒、新员工与老员工之间传承的，其中也交杂拜师学艺后的博采众长，但每个工匠及产品系列有着其独特的“秘方”，如泥料配比、工艺技巧等等，这些轻易不会外传。随着紫砂陶瓷酒瓶业迅猛发展，特别是工业化制瓶的出现，老的制瓶工艺大师的谢世，古法制瓶作坊非但没有淡出市场，而且越发的引人瞩目，新的紫砂陶瓷工艺大师崭露头角，也有年轻人甘愿耐着寂寞学习枯燥而又繁杂的技艺，宜兴金鱼紫砂陶瓷酒瓶烧造技艺也得到了较好的传承。我们进入

⑥

⑦

中华老字号

宜兴金鱼紫砂陶瓷酒瓶烧造技艺·研究方法

①②文化部非遗司专家组在宜兴市文广新局许夕华局长陪同下现场指导工作
③④⑤⑥⑦宜兴金鱼紫砂陶瓷酒瓶烧造技艺研讨会及田野考察工作现场

了金鱼陶瓷，对其工作环境进行调查，全程观察记录了紫砂陶瓷酒瓶制作的整个过程，并听取了传承人，对紫砂陶瓷酒瓶原料、工序、工具、养护、收藏、鉴赏等的详细介绍，并记录下来。期间我们通过拍摄照片、录像等手段记录了整个工艺过程，作为珍贵的资料加以分析研究。

资料整理与研究。田野调查中获得的原始资料繁杂、零乱、形式不同，呈无结构状态，道听途说等不严谨资料又掺杂其中。一方面需要去伪存真，加以鉴别，另一方面需要进行分类整理，形成有序的、有主题编码的记录资料。尤其需要注意的是非物质文化遗产具有变异特性。尤其在“意识”层面最易发生变化，社会环境变迁首先会影响人的精神意识，而行为相对滞后。对非物质文化遗产的保护，要在保存记录“载体”和“行为”的同时，还要注意经常研究其行为背后的意识因素，把物质、行为及精神意识各层面作为一个系统整体来进行资料性采录和研究，做到既能观其形，又能察其异，去体察每一项遗产事象的产生、流变，为保护其可持续发展提供借鉴。

逻辑分析。考察、采集、整理后得来的资料依旧比较散乱，难于整体反映项目状况。还需下大力气用专业的态度、科学的精神，采用逻辑分析的方法进一步研究整理这些材料，最终做出研究报告，将研究成果全面、正确地反映出来，才能形成较为系统的体系，便于人们理性地对待宜兴金鱼紫砂陶瓷酒瓶烧造技艺，让更多的人更加深入地了解、保护、传承这项宝贵的非物质文化遗产。

前景预测。根据调查的资料和分析的结果，对金鱼紫砂陶瓷酒瓶烧造技艺的发展与趋势进行预测，为其今后的发展提供借鉴和指导性帮助。我们通过对不同时代、不同特点、不同系列的产品研究，通过深入走访其相关的客户和使用者，了解其诉求的未来发展和潜在的可能，从而为金鱼紫砂陶瓷酒瓶的传承与创新提供可依据的可续资料和数据，帮助其更好地改进现有的生产工艺，在继承传统的基础上，开创出新的产品和工艺来，从而推动传统工艺的进一步发展和提升。

本次采访了数十位相关的宜兴金鱼紫砂陶瓷酒瓶烧造技艺方面的民俗文化专家、代表性传承人，采访录音长达近百小时，见证老物件数十个，收到整理的相关制作成品上百件。同时收到当地热心人士提供的线索、资料千余条，拍摄图片5000余张，最后通过逻辑分析的方法，对宜兴金鱼紫砂陶瓷酒瓶烧造技艺的保护与传承作出了研究报告。

①

②

③

④

⑤

⑥

⑦

⑧

中华老字号

宜兴金鱼紫砂陶瓷酒瓶烧造技艺·研究方法

①②③④⑤⑥⑦⑧宜兴金鱼紫砂陶瓷酒瓶烧造技艺田野考察工作现场

概述

1 宜兴蠡河码头

中华老字号

宜兴金鱼紫砂陶瓷酒瓶烧造技艺·历史渊源

一、宜兴酒器文化的历史渊源

"一脉相传，独具风流。"

我国的酿酒历史源远流长，随之而来的酒器酒具也是历史悠久，我国古代的酒器文化的发展经历了史前、夏商周时期、秦汉至南北朝时期、隋唐时期、宋辽金元时期及明清时期几个典型的阶段，宜兴的酒器发展是不外乎也经历了这几个阶段，只是在某些阶段出现了其独有的发展脉络及发展特点。

我国酿酒大约始于6000多年前新石器晚期，酒的产生带动酒具的发展，从此至夏朝建立视为酒具发展的史前时期。这一时期人类的历史从茹毛饮血的时代进入农业文明时代，粮食的剩余和陶器的诞生，实现了人类对火与土的征服，酒也在人们的日常生活中诞生。据《神农本草》记载，酒起源于远古与神农时代，《世本八种》（增订本）中记载："仪狄始作，酒醪，变五味，少康作秫酒。"说明在夏代人们已经有意识有组织地酿酒。远古时代的酒不同于现在，是未加过滤蒸馏，汁渣混在一起的糊状或半流质的酒醪，谈不上喝，吃酒所用的器具与餐具、炊具的区分还不是很明显。宜兴骆驼墩新石器时代遗址中发掘出精美的石器和陶器，甚至有加工粮食的大口缸和碳化的稻米；在宜兴西溪新石器文化遗址中也发掘出了不少陶器、陶片、釜、鼎等餐具灶具，器形有坛、罐、瓿、钵等。

随着酿酒技术的发展，酒器酒具逐渐从炊具、餐具中独立出来，到了新石器晚期，考古证明这时已经有了专门的酒器，出现了类似于后世酒具的陶器。这一时期的酒器类型增加，用途明确，与后世的酒器颇为相似，器形有罐、瓮、盂、碗、杯等；酒杯的种类也很多，有平底杯、圈足杯、高圈足杯、高柄杯、斜壁杯、曲腹杯、觚形杯等的区别。然而这一时期全国不同地区的原始文明差异较大，各地出土的文物有着浓厚的地方特色，陶酒器的器形和组合也各有不同，总体来看，这一时期的酒器已基本满足了盛、温、斟、饮等要求，但器形仍古拙淳朴，仍有深深的大自然印记，带着浓厚的泥土的气息。

时代发展至夏商周时期，我国的礼仪制度发展成熟，"礼成于酒"，无酒不成礼，祀天地、祭宗庙、奉嘉宾，各种重大礼仪无处不见酒的踪影，酒礼的复杂空前绝后。酒的高度礼遇也使得酒具飞速发展，这一时期的酒器多为高贵的青铜酒器。夏王朝继承了原始社会积累了几千年的酒文化，并有了飞跃性的发展和开拓。商代酿酒业进一步发达，酒器的品类迅速增多。西周酒器基本沿承商代旧制，东周时期瓷器发明，这时的酒器除漆器与青铜器外，瓷器的比重逐渐增加，陶酒器明显减少。《殷周青铜器通论》记载：商周的青铜器共分为食器、酒器、水器和乐器四大部，共五十类，其中酒器占二十四类。酒器按用途分为煮酒器、盛酒器、饮酒器、贮酒器，此外还有礼器，形制丰富，变化多样。这其中有很讲究的基本组合，主要是爵与觚，然而即使同一形制，在不同的历史时期其外形、风格也都有着深深的时代烙印。

中国酒器在公元前221年秦始皇一统天下后也揭开了新的一页，酒逐渐落入民间，饮用范围更加广泛，酒器也逐渐走下神坛，消除了神秘感，日益生活化。秦汉至南北朝时期中国历史一波三折，除汉代大多时间在战乱中度过，人们的思想也是极度的活跃，到了魏晋南北朝，社会思想的开放达到了东周之后的又一高潮，南京市西善桥东晋墓中出土刻砖壁画《竹林七贤图》，将这一时期嗜酒文人的神态描绘得惟妙惟肖，这样的社会思潮也深深地烙印在了酒器上。

秦汉的酒器大体沿承东周遗风，青铜酒器和漆酒器并重，西汉末年至魏晋时期，青铜酒器减少，漆酒器增多，多向活泼实用发展。民间则广泛流行陶瓷酒具。汉初酒壶的造型一般是大而有颈或者大腹长颈，且颈可系绳。西汉晚期，壶口已呈现喇叭形，双耳常作铺首衔环。东汉最盛行的酒具是盘口壶，口径较高，口内盘面很小，口颈交接处有明显的棱线，球腹平底。宜兴丁蜀镇南山北麓有座汉代的古窑址，考古人员发掘出大量陶瓷碎片及少量的完整器皿，器形有碗、盆、瓶等，是为宜兴烧造酒器的最早明证。

魏晋南北朝时期连年战争，文人苦闷，狂放不羁，多饮酒清谈，刘伶在酒赋名篇《酒德颂》说："捧罂承槽，衔杯漱醪，奋髯箕踞，枕曲藉糟，无思无虑，其乐陶陶。"这样的时代背景下皇室用具不再奢华，厚葬之风消减，酒器酒具的神秘庄严也日渐消失，生活化的风格日益突出，此时的墓葬出土的酒器也多是陶瓷制

①连珠纹爵
②二里头文化遗址
③商代早期（公元前16世纪—前15世纪）盉

品，器形包括壶、尊、杯、注子、温碗等，有鸡首壶、瓷扁壶、青瓷莲花尊、飞鸽瓷杯等等。其中早期的鸡头壶多小盘口，一面贴鸡头，一面贴鸡尾，头尾前后对称，鸡头实心；东晋时，壶身变大，前装引颈高冠鸡头，圆形把手，上端接壶口，下端接壶腹；东晋中晚期，把手的上端饰有龙头和熊纹，器形更加优美；到了南朝，壶身变得修长，口颈加高，造型实用。除鸡头壶外，这一时期的扁壶酒器也很普遍。总体看这时的酒具带有鲜明的时代特征，其总体造型风格也趋于生活化，北方曾出土兼具盛酒、温酒和饮酒三种功能的酒器，做工精良小巧，是明显的家庭实用酒器；宜兴的吴晋时期南方青瓷窑址群中发掘出许多日用器皿的碎片，其酒器有盘口壶、双系罐等，在宜兴西晋周氏墓地中也出土了50余件相类似的青瓷酒器。其制作技巧高超，造型多样，其中不乏六朝青瓷中的上品。特别是青瓷神兽尊，是为当时青瓷手工业杰作，它神态生动，酷似当时的石质辟邪，昂首张口，嘴内含珠，四爪、双翼、羽毛、脊尾清晰传神，内外遍施青灰色釉，釉色细腻、光洁、匀整、晶莹，底上有“东州”二字。经鉴定这些完整的瓷器很可能就是产自宜兴均山窑，这为陶瓷酒具在隋唐时期的突飞猛进奠定了很好的基础。

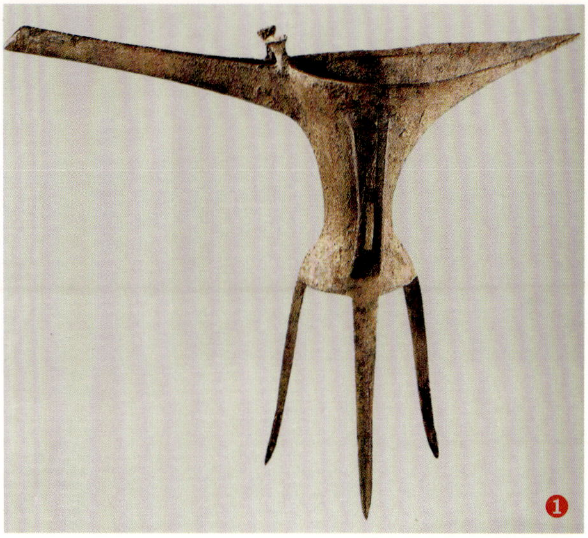
❶

❷

隋唐时期中国古代文化形成了独有的特点，酒器文化随酒文化的发展而发展，形成以瓷器为主、金银酒器为辅的新局面。隋代的酒壶大致分带流和无流两种，带流者为鸡头壶，壶身比南朝时期更瘦长，壶口加高，壶颈变细，中部多饰弦纹；不带流的为盘口壶，壶身瘦长，盘口高而微撇，壶颈长而直，腹呈椭圆形。唐代的陶瓷生产有“南青”“北白”之说，这时的瓷酒器中青瓷和白瓷酒器都负盛名。唐代的瓷制酒器品类较多，样式也极为新颖奇特，主要有联体壶、执壶、盏、注子、杯、碗、盅、双耳瓶等。诗人高适有“床头一壶高，能更几回眠”之句。唐代酒具中执壶最常见，名为注子，也叫注壶。晚唐时期出现各式小酒壶，有的形似盘口壶，有的如球形小罐，肩部装一个外壁塑成多角形的短嘴。还有的壶是一种喇叭口短颈，球腹平底，肩腹间装短嘴和手柄各一。与酒壶一同使用的是酒杯，有圈足直筒杯、带柄小杯等。五代时期，执壶的嘴变长而微曲，壶腹一般为瓜果（棱）形，柄加长，容量也有所增加。还出现了一种带西域风格的扁壶，扁圆形状，直颈、平口、梯形足。

唐初宜兴归径等地大量烧制日用青瓷，在丁蜀镇发现了中晚唐时期的涧罴窑，而在张渚区归径的棚山和真武殿山的南北麓，是晚唐五代窑群，多达数十座，两处陶瓷产品多为简朴的民间日常用品，如碗、钵、罐、盘、灯盏等，酒器更不在少数。涧罴窑的产品釉色青绿微带黄色，归径窑群的产品多为茶绿色，还有较少酱色釉。这时已采用套钵，釉面的光泽度提高，还原气氛的控制加强，所以产品的釉面呈色更显青翠温润。

❸

北宋继承隋唐酒文化遗风，其酒器的造型及装饰纹样包括饮酒习俗仍保留着深厚的汉文化底蕴，瓷酒器在酒器中占据主要领地，器形主要有经瓶、杯盏、温碗注子和倒装壶等。特别是倒装壶是宋代首创酒器。宋代“武功不足，文治有余”的社会背景反映在酒器的造型与装饰方面，也就

中华老字号

宜兴金鱼紫砂陶瓷酒瓶烧造技艺·历史渊源

如同诗词书画一样强调准确、细腻、韵味，工于新巧。辽、金、元等王朝，逐水草而居的传统反映在酒具上，便产生了适合游牧生活的酒具，如龙把鸡冠壶、葫芦形倒装壶、银马镫壶以及各种瓷扁壶等，后来受先进的汉文化浸染，其酒具也出现了青花凤首执壶及各类酒经瓶、温碗、注子等，数次于辽金墓葬中出土，沿承了宋代的瓷酒器风格，并有独特发展。元代是瓷器发展史上承前启后的关节，在中国瓷酒器发展史上具有重要地位。这时出现了釉里红高足转杯、蓝釉爵杯、青花诗文菊花杯、白釉描金高足杯等酒器，器形、釉色都有了很大提高，诗文词句装饰酒器的现象也更加广泛，酒文化的内容大大丰富。

宋辽金元时期我国的酒业规模空前壮大。宋代的酒瓶直书与酒相关的文字，更有酒店或旅馆的名称，欧阳修的《归田录》提到："仁宗在东宫，鲁肃简公为谕德，其居在宋门外，俗谓之浴堂巷，有酒肆在其侧，号'仁和'，酒名于京师，公往往易服微行，饮于其中。"宋代的日常酒具南北方各窑口都有烧制，形式多样，常见的有瓜棱壶、提梁壶等。梅瓶即在宋朝开始盛行，有的用来装酒。元代流行执壶酒具，它以玉壶春瓶为壶身，流贴附在腹上，流比宋代加长，高度一般与壶口平行，嘴向外倾斜；柄与流对称，壶口稍外撇，盖扣其上。其间，还流行多种大酒瓶和酒罐。还出现适应游牧习俗、便于马上饮酒用的高足杯。辽金元时期酒器普遍向两极化发展，贮酒器形体较大，一般用陶；饮酒器则形体渐渐缩小，材质珍贵，出现不少金银、玛瑙、水晶、玻璃等酒杯。

❶

❷

中国陶瓷业在明清两朝达到了鼎盛，官窑民窑同辉，彩绘色釉并茂。这段时期的陶瓷酒具，一反宋朝的素雅，大多通体满饰花纹，花朵、海浪、莲瓣、瑞兽等可占据酒具的主体。大酒器器形沿承宋元时期的执壶、梅瓶等形制；在元代推广蒸馏酿造技术后，酒具器形逐渐缩小。明代常见酒具有梨形壶、龙柄壶、莲瓣壶、鸡心壶、亭盖方壶等。清代的造型更丰富，品种花样繁多，更因皇帝的嗜古喜好，仿古酒器盛行。明清时期虽不断受外倭袭扰，但酒文化作为中国传统文化的重要分支，其载体酒器以其固有的强势继续向世人展示着它不朽的艺术内蕴和辉煌成就。

❸

宜兴的陶瓷酒器历来较少参与国家定制，而以民用为主，酒器为人们生活日用为主，少有贡品御器等精致的代表作，较之水具、茶具，较少专用。宜兴陶土资源算不上得天独厚，除紫砂泥，较少优质的瓷土、陶土等，同时这也成为宜兴陶瓷的独特优点，就是宜兴的陶瓷对泥土要求不严，而且都有其独到之处，而且宜兴陶土资源开发利用，在矿源开采、泥料炼制等方面，工艺不断更新提高，具有广泛的适应性、实用性和多样性。所以宜兴制陶烧瓷因地因时制宜，在当地陶土资源丰富、外地瓷土流量不

❹

①商代中期兽面纹
②西周早期象尊
③西周早期引觥
④西周中期伯饮壶
⑤单子尊
⑥蟠虺纹方鉴
⑦1981年洛阳市发现东汉古墓《夫妇宴饮图》
⑧彩色釉凤首壶
⑨执温酒注石俑

5

6

7

8

9

中华老字号

宜兴金鱼紫砂陶瓷酒瓶烧造技艺・陶瓷器具的分类

足时，则以本地陶土、陶泥为主要原料；在紫砂茶具升值、瓷土交易便捷时，又以瓷质酒具为主。自然条件的限制和宜兴的能工巧匠，使得宜兴的陶瓷善于继承和创新，比如将瓷胎与紫砂色、紫砂胎与色釉有机结合，生产出各种紫砂陶瓷酒瓶，这样紫砂陶土的价值和现代工艺价值融合一处，相得益彰，成为紫砂陶瓷文化史上又一里程碑式创造。

二、宜兴陶瓷器具的分类

“历经千年，大浪淘沙，存此精品。”

陶瓷酒器依着陶瓷的不同而出现不同的分类，所以要弄清陶瓷酒器的分类，首先需要弄清陶瓷的分类。

中国陶瓷历史悠久，陶瓷之间的界限也很模糊，分类的依据也很多。如今人们一般对陶瓷的分类有以下几种：依照陶瓷的性能分为高强度陶瓷、铁电陶瓷、耐酸陶瓷、高温陶瓷等等；按是否施釉分为有釉陶瓷和无釉陶瓷；按用途分，则有日用陶瓷、艺术（陈列）陶瓷、卫生陶瓷、建筑陶瓷、电器陶瓷、电子陶瓷、化工陶瓷、纺织陶瓷、透千（燃气输机）陶瓷等等；另外，还有依据所用原料及坯体的致密程度，分为粗陶、细陶、炻器、半瓷器、瓷器等，原料从粗到精，坯体从粗松多孔，逐步到达致密、烧结，烧成温度也是逐渐从低趋高。

粗陶是最原始最低级的陶瓷器，一般取材黏土，有时会加入熟料或砂，以减少收缩。在氧化焰中烧成会呈黄色或红色，在原焰中烧会呈现青色或黑色，一些普通的建筑砖瓦就是此类。

细陶陶器又分普通陶器和精陶器两类，普通陶器有土陶盆、罐、缸、瓮以及耐火砖等，它们具有多孔性，是着色坯体。而精陶按坯体组成的不同，分为黏土质、石灰质、长石质、熟料质四种。黏土质精陶近于普通陶器；石灰质精陶以石灰石为熔剂，近年很少生产，已被长石质精陶所取代。长石质精陶又称硬质精陶，以长石为熔剂，是陶器中最好、使用最广的一种，目前许多国家用这种陶器制作日用餐具（杯、碟、盘、盂等）及卫生陶器，以代替价格高昂的瓷器。熟料质的热料精陶是在精陶坯料中加入一定量的熟料，减少收缩，避免废品，现在多应用于大型和厚胎制品，如浴盆、大盥洗盆等。

炻器即我国古籍上所提到的“石胎瓷”，紫砂壶就是此类。它坯体致密，完全烧结，接近瓷器；但还未

①③④⑤宜兴陶都历史照片
②宜兴窑货各种价目表

玻化，仍有3%以下的吸水率，坯体不透明，烧后有白色，更多是呈现颜色，对原料纯度的要求不及瓷器那样高。炻器强度高，热稳定性良好，并能适应从冰箱到烤炉的温度急变，非常适合现代化的生活需求。半瓷器坯料接近瓷器坯料，烧后有3%～5%的吸水率，其性能介于瓷器和精陶之间。

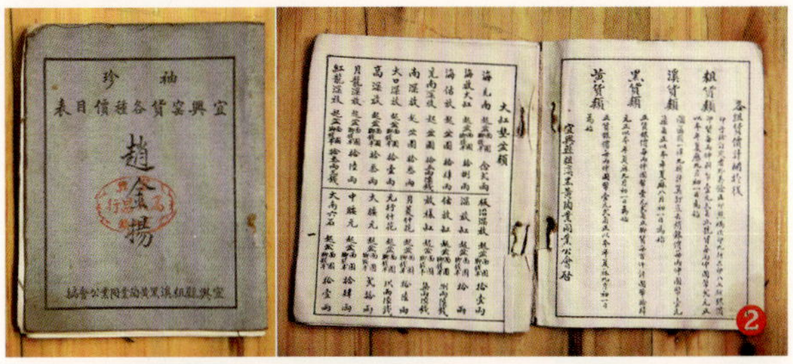

瓷器是陶瓷器发展的更高阶段，在中国出现于东汉时期。其特征为坯体已完全烧结，完全玻化，非常致密，对液体和气体都无渗透性，吸水率在0.5%以下，胎薄半透明，断面呈贝壳状，舌舔光滑而不被粘。硬质瓷在陶瓷器中性能最好，常用于制造高级日用器皿、电瓷、化学瓷等。软质瓷所含的熔剂多，烧成温度较低，机械强度和热稳定性都较低，但透明度高，富于装饰性，常用于制造艺术陈设瓷。另外，还有熔块瓷与骨灰瓷，其烧成温度及优缺点与软质瓷相近，但生产难度较大，成本较高，生产较少。

我们日常中所见到的酒器多是用粗陶、细陶、瓷器做成的，炻器由于气孔大，宜渗漏，很长时间以来基本上不用它做酒器，特别是储酒器。于是我们日常所见到的陶瓷酒器就多为粗陶酒器、细陶酒器、瓷质酒器。

这是从一般意义上的陶瓷划分来说，在宜兴则有另一种说法。由于一些大窑户身怀绝技，产品各具特色，使陶器形成了粗货、溪货、黑货、黄货、砂货、紫货6个生产区。所以酒器方面，也就有了粗货酒器、溪货酒器、黑货酒器、黄货酒器、砂货酒器、紫货酒器之说。可惜的是砂货酒器、紫货酒器一直只是个传说，停留在人们的口头上。直到谈志坚的出现，将这种传说变为了现实。从而真正实现了六大陶瓷酒器辉耀宜兴的盛景。

粗货酒器、溪货酒器、黑货酒器、黄货酒器大家比较常见，历史上广为使用和流传，所以这里不再作详述。下面我们将着重谈一下其中的砂货酒器和紫货酒器。

砂货酒器和紫货酒器很长时间以来之所以无法烧制成功，是因为它对于火候和技艺的要求十分严格，稍有不慎或者一点做得不到位就会功败垂成，这也是我们上面提到的炻器酒器一直没有的原因。谈志坚通过多年的研究和积累，终于发现了解决的办法。他通过科学的研究和分析，发现紫砂器皿渗水的根本原因在于传统的手工艺制作中不可避免的弊端和紫砂器皿烧制温度偏低等所致。所以要想解决紫砂器皿渗水的问题，就需要从这几方面入手。于是他从材料筛选、研磨、选择先进的现代工艺设备等入手，采用了在1991年用文片瓷（表面有裂纹）做酒瓶的技术，即在釉和胎之间加过渡层，从而解决了高温烧制紫砂器皿易开裂的技术难题。最终成功烧制出了紫砂陶瓷酒瓶，填补了这一历史性空白，成为宜兴陶瓷史上的一个具有里程碑意义的创举。

现在紫砂陶瓷酒瓶已被广泛地应用于各大白酒生产厂家之中，成为他们提升酒的档次，增加酒的内涵，提升酒的品质的重要手段和工具，也成为人们争相收藏的重要紫砂陶瓷艺术品之一。

中华老字号

宜兴金鱼紫砂陶瓷酒瓶烧造技艺·陶瓷器具的分类

三、宜兴陶瓷酒器的技艺传承

“沿承传统，力主创新。”

陶瓷酒器技艺的发展传承与陶瓷技艺的发展不可分割。中国陶瓷历史悠久，现存文献常有关于陶的记载，如成书于春秋时期的《考工记》中记载“凝土以为器”、“虞氏上陶”，《周书》写到“神宜耕而作陶”，《资治通鉴》记载“黄帝命宁封为陶正”，《吕氏春秋》说“黄帝有陶正昆吾作陶”，《史记》记载“舜陶于河滨”等等。历年的考古发现也证明早在新石器时代华夏祖先就以智慧和勤劳，制造各类日用陶器，烧造出各种汲水器、炊煮器和储藏器，并饰以各种纹路及堆贴、彩绘、镂空等装饰手法，其造型集实用与审美于一体，承载并延续着原始社会的灿烂的文化艺术。新时代晚期酒器与餐具的分工尚未完成，这时的陶瓷器具的材质选择不很精准，只是一般的黏土。

宜兴位于长江中下游、太湖地区，与马家浜文化一脉相承，其境内有多处新石器时代遗址，其中西溪村原始文化遗址出土了陶壶和陶罐；骆驼墩遗址发现了红陶盆、陶鼎、陶碗等。西溪遗址发掘出文物300多件，有釜、豆、罐、盆、钵、器盖、器座、支座、蒸箅、炉箅等大量陶器，大多体态硕大，造型古朴。经分析鉴定，这些陶器以夹细蚌末红陶为多，有一定数量的红衣陶、黑衣陶、褐衣陶和褐陶，陶胎较为一致，基本不见泥质陶和夹砂陶。此外，遗址还出土了许多乌黑发亮的黑衣陶、艳丽夺目的红衣陶以及惟妙惟肖的母背子羊陶塑等陶制品。这些文物的出土说明宜兴先民早已掌握烧制陶器的技艺，而且烧造的规模也已不小。

夏朝，中国的原始酿酒业步入了新的阶段，古籍对酿酒多有记载，《世本·作篇》记载“仪狄造酒”、“杜康造酒”、“少康作秫酒”。这一时期的遗址中便出现了陶质盉、觚、爵、壶、角、杯等酒器，也有不少精美的青铜酒器。据宜兴县志载，在西周时期宜兴就出现了圆形升焰窑，在这一时期的宜兴下湾遗址中曾发掘出大量陶瓷，其中以几何印纹硬陶片和原始青瓷片为主。而属西周至春秋时代的土墩墓群中，也出土了随葬的几何印纹硬陶器和原始青瓷器，几何印纹硬陶器形有坛、罐、瓿、钵等造型，原始青瓷器形有盂、盏、碗等。

历史研究和考古发现均表明，商王朝的礼仪制度达到了顶峰，而酒是礼仪的最重要部分，而酒器诸如爵、斛、觯、角、壶、觥等酒器也备受重视，常被用于祭祀盛仪和宴享重典，并成为国家礼器的显著标志。随之而来，酒礼器的制作便在商代的手工业制作中占据了重要地位，酒器产品已达到

❶

❷

❸

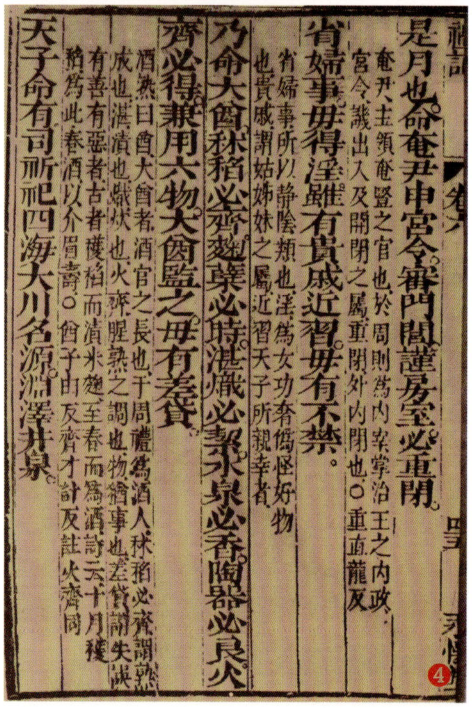
是月也，命奄尹申宮令，審門閭，謹房室，必重閉。奄尹，主領奄豎之官也，於周則為內宰，掌治王之內政、宮令，譏出入及開閉之屬。重閉，外內閉也。○重，直龍反。
省婦事，毋得淫，雖有貴戚近習，毋有不禁。省婦事所以靜陰類也。淫，謂女功奢偽怪好物也。貴戚，謂姑姊妹之屬。近習，天子所親幸者。
乃命大酋，秫稻必齊，麴糵必時，湛熾必絜，水泉必香，陶器必良，火齊必得，兼用六物，大酋監之，毋有差貸。酒熟曰酋。大酋者，酒官之長也，於周則為酒人。秫稻必齊，謂孰成也。湛，漬也。熾，炊也。火齊，腥孰之調也。物，猶事也。差貸，謂失誤，有善有惡者。古者獲稻而漬米麴，至春而為酒。詩云十月獲稻，為此春酒，以介眉壽。○酋，子由反。齊，才計反。注火齊同。
天子命有司祈祀四海、大川、名源、淵澤、井泉。
❹

①出土器物——陶瓿
②史记考证
③青瓷神兽尊
④中国酒文化
⑤⑥宜兴陶都历史照片
⑦宜兴金鱼酒瓶生产工作现场

了相当的水平，20世纪曾多次出土仍留有酒香，甚至是仍盛有古酒的青铜酒器。孔子的八世孙孔鲋在《孔丛子》提到一句古谚 “尧舜千锺，孔子百觚”。觚，就是古时一种喇叭形的盛酒器。妇好墓中就出土了一个精美的青铜方觚，以此觚为代表这里出现了大批酒具，即显示了商代饮酒风气之盛业展示了当时的酒器制造水平，很多器形延至后世，被陶瓷酒器的制作所借用。周与商一脉相承，酿酒继续繁荣，已有五齐（剂）说法，其酿酒技术已达到一定的水平。综观在商周时期的酒器，便以青铜器为主，漆酒器为主，陶酒器较为少见。战国时期的酒具数量多、而且质量很高，基本上达到瓷化，其品种有壶、杯、碗、盅、斗、爵、觥、觚、卮、角、彝、卣、盏、觯等。

秦汉时期，宜兴地区陶窑密布，盛产青釉陶，火度高，釉质硬，此为青瓷烧造的滥觞，同样是青瓷酒具的重要烧造地。在汉代，宜兴地区原始青瓷的生产已经很普遍，考古人员在丁蜀镇附近先后发现西獾墩窑、狮子墩窑、龙丫汉窑、馒头墩东窑、馒头墩西窑、马臀汉窑、新塘边汉窑、东瓦窑的一号汉窑和二号汉窑，还有风水涧窑群等多处汉窑址。这时的窑炉普遍采用圆形升焰窑，其中川埠石码头汉窑还保存了较完整古窑址，窑墙以红砖砌成，炉膛及火道仍清晰可见，保存完整为江南罕见。这时的窑炉已掌握了一定的还原气氛，其中出土的原始青瓷酒器原料选用一般瓷器所用的高岭土，器物坯体多用轮制，器形以罐、壶、瓮等为主，多饰有弦纹和水浪纹；釉色一般青绿偏黄，釉陶的坯胎断面多呈灰青色。而典型意义的青瓷酒器出现于东汉的中后期。宜兴市丁蜀镇建新村南山北麓发现一处汉代古窑遗址，从堆积物及残片分析，此窑从汉代始烧一直延亘至两晋时期。

20世纪中后期，宜兴均山地区先后发掘出10多处两晋时期的古窑址，总称为吴晋时期南方青瓷窑址群，这是我国南方早期青瓷的重要产地之一，当然更不乏青瓷酒器产品。这些六朝青瓷窑群与汉代窑址几乎重叠，其产品和窑具均这两个时期的陶瓷烧造为前后承袭。均山窑址上发现的窑墩直径达20米，高4米，窑炉为半倒焰式圆形窑，用砖和石条搭建，另有大量窑具和日用器皿的碎片，酒器的器形有盘口壶、双系罐等，上面装饰有弦纹、网纹、羽毛状纹、连珠纹、铺首甚至是花蕊等花纹，一般均里外施青黄色釉，即蟹青色，制作精细，底部露胎，胎色黄白，坯体断面致密，与汉窑中残片相比，这时的器具在泥料的选择与处理上都有了显著的进步，可能已经采用了常见的素烧，即釉烧两次烧成工艺，胎质细腻、紧致，吸水率很高。这时已经使用了叠烧法，而半倒焰式的圆形窑，又较汉代直焰式圆形窑已有明显进步，烧成温度大大提高，还原气氛也得以良好控制。

同期的宜兴六朝墓葬中也出土了一定数量的青瓷器，特别是近年来在宜兴城东南周墓墩的西晋“平西将军”周处家族墓地中出土了50余件青瓷器，其制作技巧高超，造型多样，其中不乏六朝青瓷中的上品。特别是青瓷神兽尊，是为当时青瓷手工业杰作，它神态生动，酷似当时的石质辟邪，昂首张口，嘴内含珠，四爪、双翼、羽毛、脊尾清晰传神，内外遍施

5

6

7

中华老字号

宜兴金鱼紫砂陶瓷酒瓶烧造技艺·陶瓷器具的分类

青灰色釉，釉色细腻、光洁、匀整、晶莹，底上有“东州”二字。这段时期宜兴酒器的代表便是青瓷酒器，而青瓷神兽尊便是青瓷酒器的最佳代表。经鉴定这些完整的瓷器很可能就是产自均山，这为瓷器在隋唐时期的突飞猛进奠定了很好的基础。

唐代的陶瓷生产有“南青”“北白”之说。 唐朝时期，宜兴的青瓷生产仍比较多，陶瓷多为简朴的民间日常用品，酒器品类较多，样式也极为新颖奇特，主要有联体壶、执壶、盏、注子、杯、碗、盅、双耳瓶等等，器物的原料已是经淘洗的黏土，胎质断面为浅灰或黄灰色，均用轮制拉坯成型，较为规整，器底留有旋削痕迹。归径窑群的产品多为茶绿色，还有较少酱色釉。这时已采用套钵，釉面的光泽度提高，还原气氛的控制加强，所以产品的釉面呈色更显青翠温润。唐初归径等地大量烧制青瓷外，这时的瓷器的胎质中已含有紫砂成分，说明古人已有意无意地运用了紫砂原料。宜兴的丁蜀镇发现了中晚唐时期的涧眾窑，其窑身残长28.4米，窑头宽2.3米，中段宽2.65米，尾部残缺。窑床坡度平缓，窑头前端有调节温度的空室，空室与窑腔间有挡火墙；窑床底部铺成“软底窑”。其窑具为黏土夹杂大量砂粒制成，胎质较厚，耐火温度高，有垫座、垫片、泥丁以及套钵等。垫座多是喇叭形或筒形，垫片为圆饼状，泥丁椭圆形，套钵内都装有叠烧的青瓷器。涧眾窑的产品特点是釉色青绿微带黄色。张渚区归径的棚山和真武殿山的南北麓，有数十座晚唐五代窑群。这些窑以龙窑为主，是劳动人民长期实践而创造的优良窑型，不仅将产量大大增加，也提高了窑腔的温度，改善了产品的烧结情况。现在生产陶瓷多用隧道窑，即是龙窑的改良。

宋朝开国皇帝宋太祖崇尚节俭，弃用金银玉器，杯盘碗盏全用陶瓷，一时间上行下效，全国以用陶瓷为荣，大大刺激了陶瓷业的迅猛发展。宋元时期，丁蜀与西渚一带大规模烧造日用陶和早期紫砂，酒器器形有罐、钵、缸和瓶等等，与全国的流行趋势相同，宜兴此时也生产了大量各种造型的梅瓶和倒流壶，多用来盛酒，而且在一些宋窑遗址中出土了很多成套的酒器。宜兴蠡墅羊角山有座宋代紫砂古龙窑遗址，坐落在黄龙山支脉的小山坡。从上到下有近代废窑和陶瓷残片，有从元初到清初的混合堆积层，而最下层便是早期紫砂残器的堆积，器形有壶、罐两类，而以壶为主。紫砂残片复原后成为高颈壶、矮颈壶和提梁壶，其泥色呈紫红，表里无釉。泥料比粗陶缸细腻，色泽单一，表面致密度差。这个时期的成型工艺已经有了明清

1

2

3

①白釉双腹龙柄瓶
②四系青釉盘口壶
③宋元时期执壶
④两晋时期双系青釉罐
⑤秦汉时期双耳青釉陶罐
⑥隋唐时期青瓷玉春瓶

紫砂的雏形，脱离了拉坯技法，开始使用紫砂所独有的泥片镶接法。其壶嘴、壶把和盖钮的粘接方法，则采用打洞捏塞法。而六方壶的壶颈起线，壶嘴捏塑的龙头形，壶嘴根部的菱花纹饰以及壶把上系带小孔的处理手法等，都为后来紫砂器造型风格的形成奠定了基础。

明清时期宜兴的紫砂器逐渐著名，享誉中外，大家熟知的是作为茶具的紫砂壶，岂不知宜兴也一直有以紫砂做酒器的传统。紫砂酒器有温酒器、盛酒器和饮酒器等，有各种造型的酒壶，乍看与紫砂茶壶没有什么异常，细看则发现紫砂酒器的壶口较小，因为它不用放茶叶，不需很大的口径；而紫砂酒杯更是造型多样，南京博物院收藏着一件项圣思蟠桃形紫砂杯，它是明末清初宜兴著名陶工项圣思的传世作品。其胎质细腻，色泽红润，出自宜兴窑；杯形似半剖的桃子，又以枝叶作杯把，三小桃为足；造型自然，意趣盎然；器表镌刻有七言诗两句"阆苑花前是醉乡，拈翻王母九霞觞"；署款"圣思"，钤"圣思氏"阳文方印；项圣思是与龚春、时大彬、陈用卿等齐名的宜兴著名陶工，善做紫砂器，但其作品传世极少，这件难得的存世精品，也是宜兴紫砂酒器的杰出代表。

宜兴紫砂酒器在清代产量很大，其器形有壶、杯等等，均保持着儒雅的本色，古意盎然，各种色陶也都独具创意。清末民初直至抗战，宜兴紫砂兴旺繁荣几十年，据史料记载，1919年宜兴的蜀山、丁山、汤渡和川埠一带的沿山村庄"家家制坯，户户捶泥"，全县有窑货行二十五家，各种陶窑四十余座。其中紫砂茗壶、花盆、花瓶和饮食器皿的制作集中在蜀山和川埠；龙盆、罐头等黑货集中在蠡墅；缸类集中于丁山和白宕；缸瓮类集中在汤渡。除随季节增减的临时工，窑场有工人近6000人，居民往往是全家参与制陶，或碎土，或炼泥，或徒手制坯，或户外晒坯，或研制釉料，或绘画施彩，或书画雕刻，或装坯烧窑，老幼妇孺齐上阵。然而因战争的破坏，到1945年抗战结束时，宜兴仅存陶窑64座，到1949年，又骤减到46座。

新中国成立后，国家制定"保护、发展、提高"的方针，颁布一系列恢复发展陶瓷生产的措施，陶瓷业获得重生；1957年在全国工艺美术艺人代表大会上，国家按"百花齐放、推陈出新"的方针，以适用、经济、美观为原则，制定了爱护老艺人、培养新生力量、加强专家、艺人和科技人员三结合等政策措施，使陶瓷业焕发出新的生机，宜兴的酒器生产也随之兴盛。

到了20世纪80年代，金鱼陶瓷有限公司率先全部改产中高档陶酒瓶，拓开茅台酒厂等市场后，全市才步入陶瓷酒瓶生产的快车道。金鱼陶瓷有限公司的生产最专业，发展最快，他们重新定位市场，全面改产陶酒瓶，并不惜一切，瞄准国际先进水平，全方位进行技术改造，成为国内首家采用辊道窑煤气烧成陶酒瓶的厂家，它上下温度极小，烧结程度好，外表光洁，色泽一致，既不渗酒，又避免了光对酒的反应作用；玻璃瓶导热快，陶酒瓶导热慢，它可相对保持瓶内的酒温，使酒不易变质。陶酒瓶的优异功能，越来越被酿酒企业看好，因而，采用陶酒瓶取代玻璃瓶的酒企业日益增多，业已成为发展的趋势。

4

5

6

中华老字号

宜兴金鱼紫砂陶瓷酒瓶烧造技艺·陶瓷器具的分类

四、宜兴金鱼紫砂陶瓷酒瓶烧造技艺的艺术特征

“古朴而典雅，庄重而显文化，为世人所爱。”

关于艺术，目前有种最流行，也是最简洁而又切中要害的说法，即艺术就是有意味的形式。酒瓶作为酒文化的载体，更承载着传达酒文化的使命，这些含有深沉意味的酒瓶就有了机会成为了独特的艺术。而那些有着诸多文化含量、高品位的陶瓷艺术酒瓶则成为酒瓶文化的代表者，传承着灿烂的酒瓶艺术，也成了酒文化不可或缺的贡献者。

艺术酒瓶的主要表现形式就是那些造型有趣味、特征明显、文化含量和品位较高的陶瓷酒瓶。与之对比的是现代玻璃酒瓶，虽然产量很大，也有水晶玻璃酒瓶等精品，但因缺乏历史的沉淀和文化含量，艺术品位也欠佳，很少能够位列艺术酒瓶行列。艺术酒瓶展示了一种文化现象，作为一种艺术门类是造型艺术生活化的主要表现，是酒瓶艺术家、制作者表达感情倾向的作品、精神领域的产品和滋养人类心灵的营养品，是人类社会生活文明、艺术化的结晶。

酒瓶所承载的酒瓶文化也因酒瓶的构成而展现。现代酒瓶通常有三个构成部分：一是“瓶（裸）体”部分，即酒瓶的本体，是酒瓶文化赖以存在的物质基础，由瓶口（头）、瓶颈、瓶肩、瓶腹、瓶底五部分组成。瓶口的展现形式有直口、斜口、歪口、双口、多口、防伪口等，其中直口又分为平口、丝口、盘口、盅口、撇口、敛口、方口、扁口、子母口、花瓣口、袋状口等；瓶颈有直颈、歪颈、弯颈、长颈、短颈、细颈、双颈、多颈等表现形式；瓶肩有方形、圆形、菱形、溜肩等等；瓶腹有筒腹、直腹、圆腹、扁腹等等；瓶底有平底、凹底、足底等等，不再赘述。二是酒瓶的附加部分，即酒瓶的附件。包括瓶标、开口的瓶启等。瓶标又分为底标、尾标、正标、反标、肩标、颈标、口标(在瓶盖周围)、顶标（在瓶盖顶部）、挂标、附标等。三是“文化”部，从“主体”和“附件”中派生出来，是通过物质部分展现出来的造型、色彩、书画及工艺装饰，及传达给人们的美学享受和文化熏陶。酒瓶三要素直观体现酒瓶艺术，三者互依互存，相得益彰，融合成为内涵丰富、外延广泛的酒瓶文化的系列内涵。

酒瓶文化在不同历史时期、不同地域在不同民族间有着不同表现形式和鲜明特征，它们或简陋、或复杂或朴拙、或精巧……随社会生产力的发展而发展，与科技水平同步提高而提高，工艺和材质也逐渐的丰富，也随着人们审美水平的提高而花样翻新。

❶

❷

❸

❹

①五粮液
②酒鬼
③丹泉
④⑦金鱼陶瓷酒瓶
⑤琼浆玉液
⑥古越龙山

早在新石器时代，宜兴就有陶瓷器出现，而原始的酒具便夹杂其中。而据丁蜀镇志记载，宜兴地区早在5000年前便开始烧制陶酒具，宜兴生产酒瓶的历史堪称悠久。在漫长的历史中，宜兴与全国各地一样，长期沿袭龙窑和隧道窑烧制陶瓷，由于上下温差较大，其产品结晶不一，收缩不一，满口容量不一，常常出现渗酒问题，但古代的酒多为自酿自饮式，即使是作坊生产存量也不会很多，储藏时间也不是很长，在这样的背景下，陶瓷酒具的应用限制不大。改革开放后，商品经济极大丰富，中国酒业迅猛发展，大规模长时间贮酒成为必须，陶瓷酒具便因其渗漏问题，长期却步于酒类包装的广阔市场门前，其产品仅徘徊在黄酒小厂市场，产量甚少。

陶酒瓶成为市场新宠，更离不开其深厚而丰富的文化内涵，特别适应现代的消费文化趋向。金鱼陶瓷有限公司的陶酒瓶造型千姿百态，其人物造型优美典雅，动物造型惟妙惟肖，线条造型简洁明快，植物造型栩栩如生。陶瓷酒瓶的装饰文化更是丰富多彩，有五彩缤纷的釉水，有似釉非釉的化妆土，有釉无釉相间的点彩，有粗犷雅丽的手彩，有形象逼真的浮雕，有张扬个性的色胎，有淳朴自然的喷砂，更有融书画为一体的镌刻，华贵富丽的镀膜，另有为酒厂量身打造的字面、商标、商品介绍的贴花装饰，均为天下独绝。陶酒瓶以其富有内涵的外观和饱经风霜而形成的质地，淋漓尽致地展现了酒文化的博大精深，深受酿酒行业青睐，多年来，该公司始终保持了供不应求的销售强势，并成为行业的领头羊，更为传播紫砂陶文化作出了巨大贡献！

作为国内著名的陶瓷酒瓶设计与生产品牌，“金鱼陶瓷”其作品不同于传统的普通陶瓷酒瓶，他有着陶都纯手工制作的传统技艺精华，又有现代化的技艺研发队伍和强大的设计团队，更有北大、清华等资深合作团队作为产品研发与制作的设计后盾，已实现一对一的、个性专属化的全套定制服务，这些作品再次与文化结缘，成为社会名流人士馈赠名品的首选。

“金鱼陶瓷”私藏系列，做工精美绝伦，不可复制，其独特的风格在中国陶瓷酒瓶界独树“金色”招牌，其“金鱼”标志也已成为其卓越品质与完美工艺的经典代表，引领着顶级陶瓷酒瓶的尖端消费时尚与私藏潮流。

⑤

⑥

⑦

代表作
宜興金魚紫砂陶瓷酒瓶
烧造技艺

一、宜兴金鱼紫砂陶瓷酒瓶代表作品

(一) 茅　台

MOUTAI

贵州茅台集团

53度白金酒白金窖藏

珍藏岁月，品味人生，伴随悠悠的酒香，回忆峥嵘的岁月。我们珍藏的不仅仅是酒，更是不可复制的人生体验。每当回忆往事，开启一瓶茅台白金酒个人珍藏酒，再次感受那精彩瞬间。

茅台白金酒酱香型白酒系列

MAOTAIBAIJINJIUJIANGXIANGXINGBAIJIUXILIE

产品：茅台名将【八一纪念经典珍藏】

客户：贵州茅台酒股份有限公司

材质：挂釉紫砂陶瓷

名将传奇 红色经典

产品：茅台名将【成就梦想2008】

客户：贵州茅台酒股份有限公司

材质：挂釉紫砂陶瓷

产品：名将1688

客户：贵州茅台酒股份有限公司

材质：挂釉紫砂陶瓷

产品：茅台名将【八一纪念经典珍藏】

客户：贵州茅台酒股份有限公司

材质：挂釉紫砂陶瓷

产品：750ml许世友名将

客户：贵州茅台酒股份有限公司

材质：挂釉紫砂陶瓷

产品：名将750

客户：贵州茅台酒股份有限公司

材质：挂釉紫砂陶瓷

产品：1L茅台名将

客户：贵州茅台酒股份有限公司

材质：挂釉紫砂陶瓷

酱香型白酒
名門
酒
贵州茅台酒股份有限公司出品
PRODUCE OF KWEICHOW MOUTAI CO.,LTD
酒精度:53%vol
净含量:500ml

产品：茅台【名门系列】

客户：贵州茅台酒股份有限公司

材质：挂釉紫砂陶瓷

琼花御液
御品
琼花御液

产品：茅台【琼浆玉液系列】

客户：贵州茅台酒股份有限公司

材质：挂釉紫砂陶瓷

MOUTAI
華窖
酒
酒精度：53%vol 净含量：500ml
贵州茅台酒股份有限公司出品
PRODUCE OF KWEICHOW MOUTAI CO.,LTD.

产品：茅台【华窖系列】

客户：贵州茅台酒股份有限公司

材质：挂釉紫砂陶瓷

产品：茅台【一品天下　28年】

客户：贵州茅台酒股份有限公司

材质：挂釉紫砂陶瓷

产品：茅台名将【全国人大会议中心　特供】

客户：贵州茅台酒股份有限公司

材质：挂釉紫砂陶瓷

产品：茅台【军城系列】

客户：贵州茅台酒股份有限公司

材质：挂釉紫砂陶瓷

产品：茅台【温酒器】

客户：贵州茅台酒股份有限公司

材质：挂釉紫砂陶瓷

产品：茅台【习酒　15年】

客户：贵州茅台酒股份有限公司

材质：挂釉紫砂陶瓷

产品：茅台习酒【醇醴经典】

客户：贵州茅台酒股份有限公司

材质：挂釉紫砂陶瓷

产品：茅台习酒【醇醴　10年】

客户：贵州茅台酒股份有限公司

材质：挂釉紫砂陶瓷

产品：茅台习酒【醇醴　10年】

客户：贵州茅台酒股份有限公司

材质：挂釉紫砂陶瓷

产品：贵州茅台酒

客户：贵州茅台酒股份有限公司

材质：挂釉紫砂陶瓷

产品：茅台1680

客户：贵州茅台酒股份有限公司

材质：挂釉紫砂陶瓷

产品：茅台醇

客户：贵州茅台酒股份有限公司

材质：紫砂陶瓷

产品：贵州茅台酒【盛世国藏】

客户：贵州茅台酒股份有限公司

材质：挂釉紫砂陶瓷

产品：贵州茅台酒【世纪经典】

客户：贵州茅台酒股份有限公司

材质：挂釉紫砂陶瓷

产品：贵州茅台酒

客户：贵州茅台酒股份有限公司

材质：挂釉紫砂陶瓷

产品：贵州茅台酒【560特制陈酿】

客户：贵州茅台酒股份有限公司

材质：挂釉紫砂陶瓷

（二）五粮液

YIBIN CO.,LTD
50
AGE 50 YEARS

产品：五粮液原度封藏68度

客户：宜宾五粮液股份有限公司

材质：挂釉紫砂陶瓷

产品：五粮液大道和谐

客户：宜宾五粮液股份有限公司

材质：青釉紫砂陶瓷

产品：礼盒装五粮液

客户：宜宾五粮液股份有限公司

材质：挂釉紫砂陶瓷

五粮液®酒
CHINESE FAMOUS TRADE MARK
60
酒精度: 60%vol
净含量: 500mL

产品：五粮液【10年】

客户：宜宾五粮液股份有限公司

材质：挂釉紫砂陶瓷

产品：五粮液【15年】

客户：宜宾五粮液股份有限公司

材质：挂釉紫砂陶瓷

产品：五粮液龙生九子

客户：宜宾五粮液股份有限公司

材质：挂釉紫砂陶瓷

50
五粮液
WULIANGYE

产品：五粮液【50年】

客户：宜宾五粮液股份有限公司

材质：挂釉紫砂陶瓷

产品：五粮液【30年】

客户：宜宾五粮液股份有限公司

材质：挂釉紫砂陶瓷

产品：五粮液【60年】

客户：宜宾五粮液股份有限公司

材质：挂釉紫砂陶瓷

五粮液®
WULIANGYE
宜宾五粮液股份有限公司
WULIANGYE YIBIN CO.,LTD.
45

产品：45度五粮液系列

客户：宜宾五粮液股份有限公司

材质：挂釉紫砂陶瓷

产品：五粮液部队特供系列

客户：宜宾五粮液股份有限公司

材质：挂釉紫砂陶瓷

产品：五粮液【国防大学】

客户：宜宾五粮液股份有限公司

材质：挂釉紫砂陶瓷

产品：五粮液【龙人龙酒】

客户：宜宾五粮液股份有限公司

材质：挂釉紫砂陶瓷

产品：五粮液【1580 十年】

客户：宜宾五粮液股份有限公司

材质：挂釉紫砂陶瓷

产品：45度五粮液系列

客户：宜宾五粮液股份有限公司

材质：挂釉紫砂陶瓷

产品：五粮液【珍品】

客户：宜宾五粮液股份有限公司

材质：挂釉紫砂陶瓷

产品：五粮液【金榜题名】

客户：宜宾五粮液股份有限公司

材质：挂釉紫砂陶瓷

产品：五粮液【60周年国庆】

客户：宜宾五粮液股份有限公司

材质：挂釉紫砂陶瓷

五粮液®
金玉满堂
酒精度：52%vol
净含量：1.8L

产品：五粮液【金玉满堂】

客户：宜宾五粮液股份有限公司

材质：挂釉紫砂陶瓷

产品：五粮液【1580 十五年】

客户：宜宾五粮液股份有限公司

材质：挂釉紫砂陶瓷

产品：五粮液【68典藏】

客户：宜宾五粮液股份有限公司

材质：挂釉紫砂陶瓷

五粮液
浓香型白酒
WULIANGYE
WULIANGYE YIBIN CO.,LTD
68
宜宾五粮液股份有限公司
酒精度:68%vol 净含量:500mL

产品：五粮液【原度封陈68度】

客户：宜宾五粮液股份有限公司

材质：挂釉紫砂陶瓷

产品：五粮液礼盒装系列

客户：宜宾五粮液股份有限公司

材质：挂釉紫砂陶瓷

产品：五粮液礼盒装系列

客户：宜宾五粮液股份有限公司

材质：挂釉紫砂陶瓷

产品：五粮液【圣酒珍藏装】

客户：宜宾五粮液股份有限公司

材质：挂釉紫砂陶瓷

产品：五粮液【部队专用酒】

客户：宜宾五粮液股份有限公司

材质：挂釉紫砂陶瓷

产品：五粮液【武警专用酒】

客户：宜宾五粮液股份有限公司

材质：挂釉紫砂陶瓷

产品：五粮液【五粮春】

客户：宜宾五粮液股份有限公司

材质：挂釉紫砂陶瓷

产品：金六福【中国红】

客户：宜宾五粮液股份有限公司

材质：挂釉紫砂陶瓷

产品：五粮液【六百岁】

客户：宜宾五粮液股份有限公司

材质：挂釉紫砂陶瓷

产品：五粮液【特供 专用 1318】

客户：宜宾五粮液股份有限公司

材质：挂釉紫砂陶瓷

（三）口子窖

真实窖藏
20
KOUZIJIAO LIQUOR AGE 20 YEARS
于芳华灼灼的此刻，追溯岁月的印记
阅历年华，只为此刻绽放
中国驰名商标
纯粮固态发酵白酒
中华老字号

产品：传世口子酒

客户：安徽口子酒业股份有限公司

材质：紫砂陶瓷

产品：传阅口子窖

客户：安徽口子酒业股份有限公司

材质：挂釉紫砂陶瓷

产品：口子窖20年

客户：安徽口子酒业股份有限公司

材质：挂釉紫砂陶瓷

产品：口子窖5年系列

客户：安徽口子酒业股份有限公司

材质：紫砂陶瓷

产品：口子窖10年

客户：安徽口子酒业股份有限公司

材质：紫砂陶瓷

产品：口子酒

客户：安徽口子酒业股份有限公司

材质：紫砂陶瓷

产品：精制口子窖

客户：安徽口子酒业股份有限公司

材质：挂釉紫砂陶瓷

口子窖
特制

产品：口子窖北京特供

客户：安徽口子酒业股份有限公司

材质：紫砂陶瓷

老口子
酒

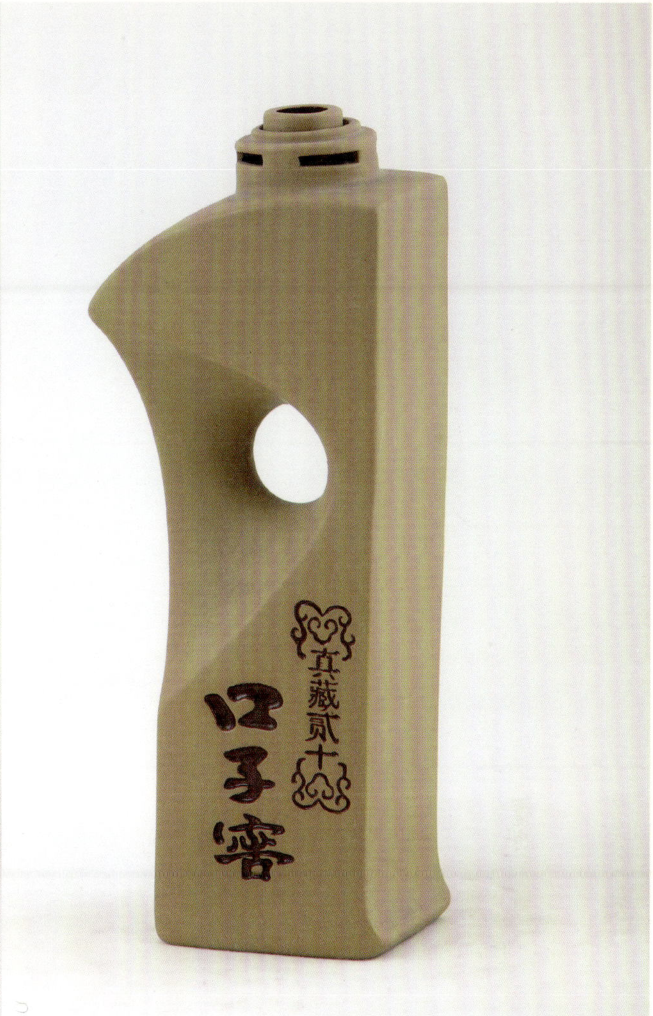
口子窖

老口子

老口子

产品：口子窖

客户：安徽口子酒业股份有限公司

材质：挂釉紫砂陶瓷

产品：口子系列

客户：安徽口子酒业股份有限公司

材质：紫砂陶瓷

（四）郎 酒

产品：军供郎酒

客户：四川郎酒集团有限责任公司

材质：挂釉紫砂陶瓷

产品：郎酒总理府系列

客户：四川郎酒集团有限责任公司

材质：挂釉紫砂陶瓷

总理府
酒
郎
ZONG LI FU
总理府
酒
郎
【中国驰名商标】
ZONG LI FU
迎宾
RECEPTION

产品：新郎酒【12年】

客户：四川郎酒集团有限责任公司

材质：挂釉紫砂陶瓷

产品：新郎酒【9年】

客户：四川郎酒集团有限责任公司

材质：挂釉紫砂陶瓷

（五）西 凤

西鳳酒®
陕西西凤酒股份有限公司
SHAANXI XIFENGJIU GUFEN YOUXIANGONGSI
酒精度：52%vol
净含量：500ml
白酒

产品：西凤酒【大酒海5L坛】

客户：陕西西凤酒股份有限责任公司

材质：挂釉紫砂陶瓷

中国名酒
西鳳酒
陕西西凤酒集团股份有限公司
SHAANXI XIFENGJIUJITUAN GUFEN YOUXIANGONGSI
酒精度:45%vol 净含量:500mL

产品：西凤酒【凤香典范 2008纪念版】

客户：陕西西凤酒股份有限公司

材质：挂釉紫砂陶瓷

产品：西凤酒【金藏 10年 20年 30年】

客户：陕西西凤酒股份有限责任公司

材质：挂釉紫砂陶瓷

西鳳酒
金藏
20
年
中国 名酒
西鳳酒
金藏
30
年
净含量:500mL 酒精度:45%voL
陕西西凤酒集团股份有限公司

产品：西凤酒【五十年 陈酿】

客户：陕西西凤酒股份有限责任公司

材质：挂釉紫砂陶瓷

产品：西凤酒【兵马俑】

客户：陕西西凤酒股份有限责任公司

材质：挂釉紫砂陶瓷

产品：国宴西凤酒

客户：陕西西凤酒股份有限责任公司

材质：挂釉紫砂陶瓷

产品：百年西凤【1915】

客户：陕西西凤酒股份有限公司

材质：挂釉紫砂陶瓷

产品：百年西凤【酒器】

客户：陕西西凤酒股份有限责任公司

材质：挂釉紫砂陶瓷

产品：西凤酒【三六九】

客户：陕西西凤酒股份有限责任公司

材质：挂釉紫砂陶瓷

产品：西凤酒【50年】

客户：陕西西凤酒股份有限责任公司

材质：挂釉紫砂陶瓷

产品：西凤开坛【文财神】

客户：陕西西凤酒股份有限责任公司

材质：挂釉紫砂陶瓷

产品：西凤开坛【武财神】

客户：陕西西凤酒股份有限责任公司

材质：挂釉紫砂陶瓷

（六）汾　酒

产品：国藏汾酒

客户：山西汾酒厂股份有限公司

材质：挂釉紫砂陶瓷

产品：汾酒【20年陈酿】

客户：山西汾酒厂股份有限公司

材质：挂釉紫砂陶瓷

产品：玫瑰汾酒【露酒】

客户：山西汾酒厂股份有限公司

材质：挂釉紫砂陶瓷

产品：汾酒20年1L

客户：山西汾酒厂股份有限公司

材质：紫砂陶瓷

产品：汾酒紫砂瓶

客户：山西汾酒厂股份有限公司

材质：紫砂陶瓷

（七）剑南春

产品：金剑南

客户：四川省绵竹剑南春酒厂有限公司

材质：挂釉紫砂陶瓷

产品：壶中岁月

客户：四川省绵竹剑南春酒厂有限公司

材质：挂釉紫砂陶瓷

产品：剑南春【玉尊】

客户：四川省绵竹剑南春酒厂有限公司

材质：挂釉紫砂陶瓷

产品：剑南春【十龄陈坛】

客户：四川省绵竹剑南春酒厂有限公司

材质：挂釉紫砂陶瓷

产品：剑南春【剑南国宝】

客户：四川省绵竹剑南春酒厂有限公司

材质：挂釉紫砂陶瓷

（八）泸州老窖

产品：国窖1573【定制酒】

客户：中国·泸州老窖股份有限公司

材质：挂釉紫砂陶瓷

FERMENTED IN
NATIONAL CELLAR 1573
CUSTOM WINE
国窖1573
定制酒

国窖1573定制酒

因您而生的极致品味艺术

产品：国窖1573

客户：中国·泸州老窖股份有限公司

材质：挂釉紫砂陶瓷

产品：国玺酒

客户：中国·泸州老窖股份有限公司

材质：挂釉紫砂陶瓷

产品：国窖1573封坛　2.5L坛

客户：中国·泸州老窖股份有限公司

材质：挂釉紫砂陶瓷

产品：国窖1573【定制酒】

客户：泸州老窖股份有限公司

材质：挂釉紫砂陶瓷

FERMENTED IN
NATIONAL CELLAR 1573
CUSTOM WINE
國窖1573
定制酒

产品：国窖1573【瓦当四尊珍藏酒　青龙】
客户：中国·泸州老窖股份有限公司
材质：挂釉紫砂陶瓷

产品：国窖1573【瓦当四尊珍藏酒　白虎】
客户：中国·泸州老窖股份有限公司
材质：挂釉紫砂陶瓷

产品：国窖1573【瓦当四尊珍藏酒　朱雀】

客户：中国·泸州老窖股份有限公司

材质：挂釉紫砂陶瓷

产品：国窖1573【瓦当四尊珍藏酒　玄武】

客户：中国·泸州老窖股份有限公司

材质：挂釉紫砂陶瓷

产品：60度国窖1573

客户：中国·泸州老窖股份有限公司

材质：挂釉紫砂陶瓷

产品：国窖1573至圣

客户：中国·泸州老窖股份有限公司

材质：挂釉紫砂陶瓷

产品：国窖1573典藏

客户：中国·泸州老窖股份有限公司

材质：挂釉紫砂陶瓷

产品：国窖1573典藏

客户：中国·泸州老窖股份有限公司

材质：挂釉紫砂陶瓷

产品：568ml国窖1573典藏

客户：中国·泸州老窖股份有限公司

材质：挂釉紫砂陶瓷

产品：国窖1573红爵

客户：中国·泸州老窖股份有限公司

材质：挂釉紫砂陶瓷

产品：泸州老窖【封坛年份酒】

客户：中国·泸州老窖股份有限公司

材质：挂釉紫砂陶瓷

产品：老窖世家

客户：中国·泸州老窖股份有限公司

材质：挂釉紫砂陶瓷

产品：泸州老窖【典藏】

客户：中国·泸州老窖股份有限公司

材质：挂釉紫砂陶瓷

产品：泸州福【典藏18】

客户：中国·泸州老窖股份有限公司

材质：挂釉紫砂陶瓷

产品：泸州老窖【世纪荣耀1915—2015】

客户：中国·泸州老窖股份有限公司

材质：挂釉紫砂陶瓷

产品：泸州老窖【典藏】

客户：中国·泸州老窖股份有限公司

材质：紫砂陶瓷

产品：泸州老窖【紫砂陶大曲】

客户：中国·泸州老窖股份有限公司

材质：挂釉紫砂陶瓷

产品：泸州老窖紫砂陶装

客户：中国·泸州老窖股份有限公司

材质：紫砂陶瓷

产品：泸州老窖【公元一九七八年封坛】

客户：中国·泸州老窖股份有限公司

材质：挂釉紫砂陶瓷

产品：泸州古酒

客户：中国·泸州老窖股份有限公司

材质：挂釉紫砂陶瓷

产品：永盛烧坊

客户：中国·泸州老窖股份有限公司

材质：紫砂陶瓷

产品：国密董酒

客户：中国·泸州老窖股份有限公司

材质：挂釉紫砂陶瓷

产品：泸州老窖【大曲酒】

客户：中国·泸州老窖股份有限公司

材质：挂釉紫砂陶瓷

产品：泸州老窖【浓香经典】

客户：中国·泸州老窖股份有限公司

材质：挂釉紫砂陶瓷

产品：泸州老窖【纪年酒】

客户：中国·泸州老窖股份有限公司

材质：挂釉紫砂陶瓷

产品：泸州福【10年】

客户：中国·泸州老窖股份有限公司

材质：挂釉紫砂陶瓷

产品：泸州老窖【双国宝纪年酒】

客户：中国·泸州老窖股份有限公司

材质：挂釉紫砂陶瓷

中华老字号

宜兴金鱼紫砂陶瓷酒瓶烧造技艺·设计要点解析

二、金鱼紫砂陶瓷酒瓶造型设计要点解析

早在七千多年以前，“昔者帝女令仪狄作酒而美，进之禹”，“古者少康林酒”，“少康，杜康也”。使得夏朝和商汤时代酒风大盛，动辄“酌以大斗，以祈黄耇”。《淮南子·主术》也说是“周礼集醒在堂，澄酒在下”。于是人们在群饮、豪饮品尝美酒之际，也瞩目于酒器的造型艺术。因为他们认为“既醉以酒，既饱以德”，德色赋以器。

酒器与人们的生活方式及在陶冶餐饮气氛等方面有着特别的作用，因而在酒瓶设计当中附加了更多人文的因素。即使再简易的一个酒瓶，也不能简单地定位为满足使用功能即可，要花更多的精力去了解和分析消费者的消费心理，酒的特点及其所代表的文化内涵。只有在基本的使用功能和附加的精神性功能都得到了很好的满足，才能算得上是一件完整的设计。

紫砂陶瓷酒瓶作为批量化工业产品，有着产品的基本属性，离不开功能、结构、材料和工艺等因素的影响。金鱼紫砂陶瓷酒瓶以其独创性的生产加工工艺、大胆创新的酒瓶造型设计而声名远播。

（一）美学特征

1．造型

如同书法讲究文房四宝，饮茶讲究茶具配套一样，中国人历来讲究“美食不如美器”，人们饮酒时不仅讲究对象、环境、时令，而且讲究酒器的精美与否、适宜与否。

酒瓶的构造，大致是由瓶口(头)、瓶颈、瓶肩、瓶腹、瓶底等部分组成。酒瓶是否美观，很大程度上取决于造型，一个造型美观的瓶子，其点、线、势、气韵等要素的处理要非常的到位，这不只是一种技术活动，而且也是一种艺术活动，以实现实用性和艺术性的完美结合。金鱼紫砂陶瓷酒瓶的造型设计主要从以下三个方面为出发点：

（1）民族特色

中国是个文明古国，拥有深厚的文化底蕴，传统的工艺美术也有着精湛的技艺和独特的风格。这些已在中华大地发展了几百年至几十个世纪，有很强的生命力，是中华民族引以为自豪的瑰宝。金鱼陶瓷将这笔丰富珍贵的文化遗产发扬光大，将其贯穿到酒瓶的设计中，开发出众多有中国特色的酒瓶造型。采用了诸如编钟、古城墙等非常有代表性的传统元素，经过提炼、综合，对具体的形象加以抽象处理。同时对产品的使用场合及消费者心理加以考虑，在配色和形态的处理上都经过仔细的琢磨，以期能达到保证功能，又不丧失美感，同时具有明显的中国民族特色。如：湖南省的“酒鬼”酒的酒瓶，造型为麻布袋，一根红绳捆扎麻袋口，古朴粗犷，非常别致，据说是仿照清代麻袋形酒壶，这是土家族著名画家黄永玉先生设计的，从中可以看出古代酒器可以成为现代酒器设计巨大的灵感来源。

（2）现代几何形态

几何元素多样，通过组合演绎还可以演变成的其他形态，这些形态线条简单、秀丽，可以产生丰富的变化，是现代主义设计的精髓。国际上很多经典的设计采用这种元素，有其独特的美感和韵味，很多经典的酒瓶设计就采用了这些现代造型设计元素，获得了很好的市场效果。酒瓶本身就是一个装饰性很强的产品，利用几何造型的元素为视觉装饰服务，可以取得出奇制胜的变化效果和强烈的视觉冲击力。设计师主要采用有圆形、椭圆形、方形等基本形态和通过变化产生的异形体，这些形态与酒瓶的功能有着直接的关联，在保证酒瓶的基本功能的条件下产生变化、达到协调，形成特殊的美感。

（3）自然形态

从自然界万物中寻找最纯粹的形式，在吸取自然精髓的情况下抽象自然形式为我所用。同时自然物象的建构秩序也是设计形式的重要演化资源。移植自然的某些关系，进而把自然物的功能和构造演绎为人为的有用的实用价值的设计物，并获得形式意义。出于兼顾产品的功能考虑，采用了葫芦、树干等自然形态，以其为基础加以造型语言化，形成独特风格形态，有着质朴清新的韵味。

2．装饰手法

在产品装饰上赋予的文化丰富多彩，有五彩缤纷的釉水装饰、千姿百态的浮雕装饰、融书画为一体的镌刻装饰、粗犷雅丽的手彩装饰、似釉非釉的化妆土装饰、有釉无釉的点彩装饰，还有酒厂特需并提供字画、商标、商品介绍的贴花装饰，以及富丽堂皇的镀膜装饰，特别是为茅台酒厂生产的陶纹片装饰酒瓶更充分体现了陶文化和酒文化的完美结合，堪称世界一绝。文化高品位的陶酒瓶引导了传统酒包装的革命，使该厂牢牢把握了市场竞争的先机。

（二）材质工艺特征

丁蜀镇及周边山区蕴藏着极其丰富的陶土资源，有硬性的甲泥、软性的嫩泥，有白泥、黄泥、紫泥、绿泥，这些矿土所含的化学元素不同，所以，在制作陶酒瓶时，必须考虑产品的特殊要求而选择不同的原料配比，紫砂陶瓷酒瓶的原材料无毒、无味，满足作为生活用具的基本要求。陶瓷具有一定的透气性，在陈酿过程中，对酒有很好的催陈效果，泥料中所含元素也有助于白酒的老熟，有益于人体；另外它有保持酒质的优势，酒对温度特别的敏感，紫砂陶瓷瓶导热慢，可相对保持瓶中的酒温，使酒不易变质；陶质瓶不透光，避免了光对酒的影响；陶瓷的渗透性小，密封性好，耐腐蚀性强，金鱼陶瓷独有的内壁挂釉技术能避免酒的挥发和化学反应；同时上釉陶瓷还有造型典雅、釉面光滑，便于拭洗等优点。这些特点充分说明以陶瓷为酒瓶材质是非常可行和适合的。

（三）文化特征

酒与酒器本身是属于物质的，但与之并存的一系列有关的文学、艺术、习俗、礼仪等都属于上层建筑中意识形态的东西，是一种文化现象，它与社会的政治、经济、军事、文化和人民的生活都有着广泛的联系。设计是社会物质生活方式的一种创造性活动，人的一切生活方式都是人类文化的体现，设计是一种文化的表达，让消费者不单是在消费物质，同时更能领会到更深层次的东西，这正是金鱼酒瓶设计时重点考虑的问题。酒瓶设计本身附带了强烈的文化信息，即借助于文化的传承力量，又要充分考虑到宗教信仰因素、传统文化因素和设计价值因素等的影响。紫砂陶瓷酒瓶的许多设计集绘画、书法、风情典故、陶艺、酒艺等于一体，是一种特殊的工艺品。随着人类文明的脚步，人类的生活在动态的变化过程中朝着物质日益丰富、生活更加艺术化的方向演进，人们更加主张现代生活与自然和谐的主体观念。现在很多消费者已经意识到其价值，已经不单单将其作为一个容器来看待，更加注重其文化内涵，加以收藏。

研究古代盛酒器的寓意能对紫砂陶瓷酒瓶设计找到更具民族性、更准确的定位，金鱼紫砂陶瓷酒瓶设计汲取传统文化的营养，得到创造性的设计。如婚庆上的白酒酒瓶的设计就利用中国一些传统的吉祥图案和造型使酒瓶所表达出来的吉祥寓意与婚庆的喜气融为一体。再如名酒汾酒瓶上的主要位置有一个“汾”字，与篆刻“酒”字融为一体，瓶上佩有《千家诗》的缩影本，情趣盎然，散发着浓郁的传统文化气息，显示出古老东方文化神奇的风韵；百年皖酒外观分黄、褐两种颜色，风格古朴凝重又不失典雅华贵，酒瓶质地光润细腻，叩之其声如铃似钟，具有相当的艺术欣赏价值，会让人有“未醉于酒，先醉于器”的感叹。

（四）金鱼紫砂陶瓷酒瓶造型设计个案分析

1. 方酒鬼——大师

充满自然洒脱之气，整体运用扎实粗犷的线条，勾勒出酒瓶的性格。通透的圆孔成为点睛之笔，凸显瓶身表面的精致，同时也是出于人性化方面的考虑，利于抓握的方便和安全。瓶盖使用木质材料，手感细腻，花纹和色泽给人温暖的感觉，瓶身与瓶盖上下冷暖对比，造型一气呵成，产生视觉上的趣味性，精致的细节体现出设计的功力。木柄盖的弧线与瓶口上下呼应，流畅的弧线和细腻的表面处理符合手部触感要求，自然古朴的气息通过手感传达出来。瓶体使用表面磨砂处理，与瓶盖木质的光滑形成质感上的反差。文字装饰更显细腻深沉的文化气质。

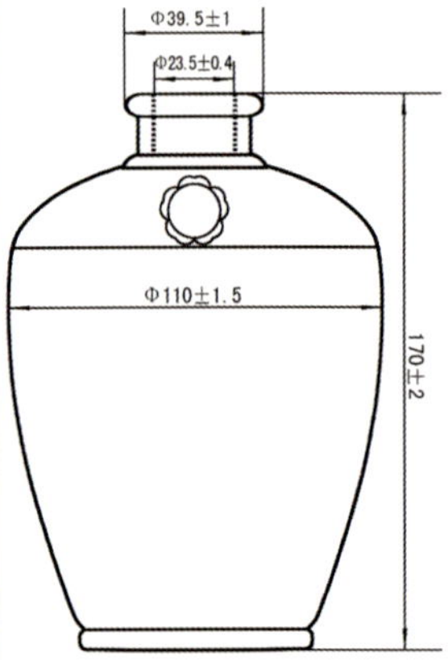

2. 国藏汾酒

造型饱满圆润，精致的裂纹釉瓷质和线条的舒缓变化，营造出高贵精细的品质性格。使用中国传统酒坛的造型，可以保证最小的体积储存足够分量的酒，降低储存空间，在运输和包装中可以降低成本。瓶盖使用美妙曲线组合，搭配整个瓶子的风格走势。瓶口处为了呼应瓶盖同样留有外凸，这样不仅有造型的考虑，同样也适合手提。瓶颈与瓶体的结合过渡与底座形成呼应，造型连贯。在表面材质处理上采用周身冰裂、裂而不破、变化万端、纹片大小相同的工艺效果，充分体现了陶文化和酒文化的完美结合。底座外凸有利于瓶体的稳固性，一条圆环增加了生动的装饰性，视觉上不会觉得单调。表面使用烫金字呼应瓶颈的金花质防伪圆环，提升了酒瓶的视觉效果。

3. 国窖1573

其造型运用粗犷的线条元素，刚硬、方正有力、沉稳大气。黑色粗糙的紫砂材质强化出酒瓶非凡的艺术效果。犹如刚毅的勇士傲然屹立，又如将军的甲胄坚不可摧。设计者巧妙地将这种感觉移植到酒瓶的设计上，使造型具有了文化隐喻特征。以色彩、肌理和平面造型等符号融通了酒文化与特定的人文观念。瓶体上由理性的矩形方块分割，配以规律的点、线、面相互结合，具有强烈的构成感和夸张的形式感。瓶盖采用与瓶体相同立方体造型，造型语言统一，在瓶盖上印有古老诗句，彰显酒瓶的文化气质。

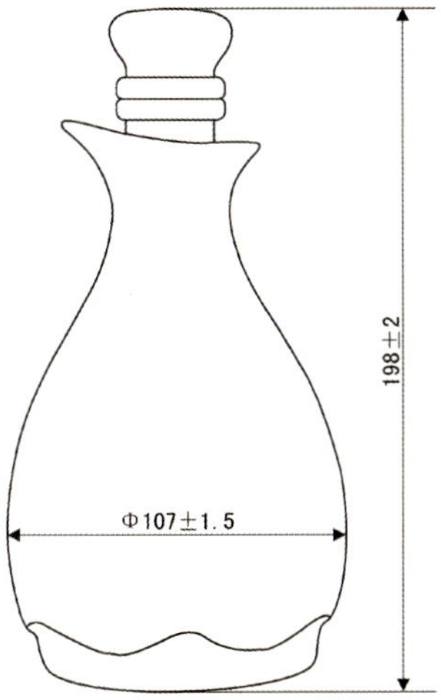

4．剑南春——壶中岁月酒壶

此酒瓶的造型以柔和变幻的曲线为主，体形饱满，在紫砂材质上附有红黑渐变的彩釉，创造出喜庆愉悦的气氛。壶底装饰有波浪形造型结构，增强了酒瓶的节奏感和韵律感，造型层次分明，在传统的酒瓶外形上融入了现代装饰的气息。壶口的设计打破了左右对称的造型，是对古老酒器造型文化继承发扬的结果，此造型不仅使酒瓶轻盈优雅，同时对斟酒这一动作进行了动作引导，有利于产品使用语意的传达，使用时酒从壶口缓缓流出，如同潺潺流水，体现东方人含蓄内敛的价值观。壶盖圆润大方，与壶口的弧线相协调，高贵的官帽造型点缀在酒瓶的顶端。洒金的图案布满壶体，更具东方特色，尽显高贵气质。

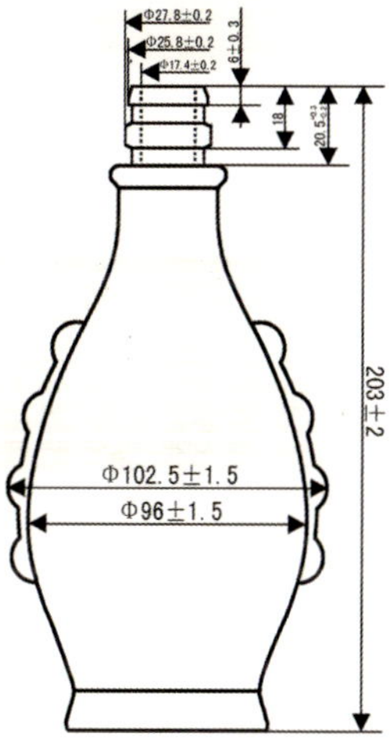

5．金六福——金缘春酒瓶

酒瓶整体为橄榄形，瓶口特意向上延长，既增加了酒瓶的形式美感，又降低了酒瓶的重心，增加了稳定性。细长的瓶口在使用时也更为舒适，功能与外观高度协调，美感与实用兼具。材质上选用不加修饰的紫砂，视觉上酒瓶古朴厚重，具有年代感。而紫砂的特性又使得酒瓶的触感非常的细腻，接触时视觉与触感强烈反差，大大增添了酒瓶的魅力。酒瓶大量装饰有古代青铜鼎上常用的夔龙纹，而瓶体两侧的装饰又似古代编钟，朴实大气，似乎能感受到强烈厚重的文化底蕴。在造型语言的运用上强调了使用和认知功能，并以隐喻和联想的方式体现了审美功能。

中华老字号

宜兴金鱼紫砂陶瓷酒瓶烧造技艺·造型设计个案分析

6．口子窖

第一次看见它不应该用酒瓶来描述它，也许用花瓶更符合一点。高挑优雅，运用水滴的造型表现整体流畅感觉，是幽幽醇香、滴水甘露的寓意所在。犹如一滴香浓的酒水滴落在空中凝固了下来，将它的香气美味同样凝聚瓶子里，寓意酒质纯粹。瓶盖与瓶体的螺旋纹层层交叠，犹如涟漪一样从水的中央慢慢扩散开来，在与瓶颈的曲势形成整体动势，有扩散、飘荡之意。层叠造型与瓶颈单纯圆柱造型形成动静对比，形成繁简结合的韵律美感，像一首美妙的音乐有节奏的跳动。

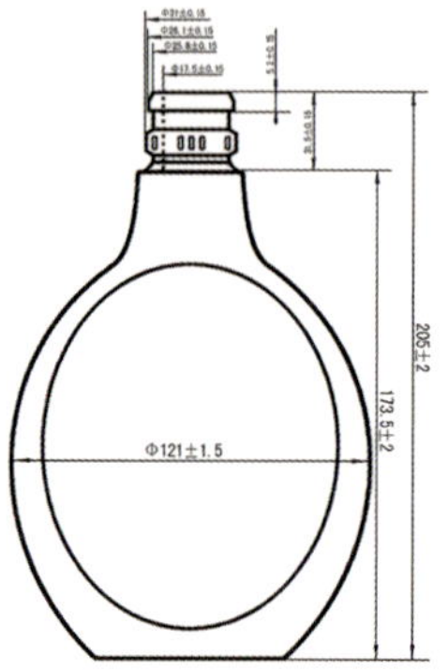

7．新郎酒

成熟、尊贵。整体的形状借鉴异域酒包装特征，沉稳的藏蓝色给人以成熟稳重的感觉，加上顶部的金色装饰图案，形成贵族气质。瓶盖成为整个瓶子的亮点，顶部的瓶盖设计成珠宝的造型，显示酒瓶的高贵。瓶盖周围使用古典的雕文装饰，并且使用了英文图案，更加强调了酒瓶的异国情调。整体线条顺畅、造型搭配合理，使用扁平瓶体适合手拿。前后标贴使用烫金效果，勾勒出瓶子造型的形式美感特征。

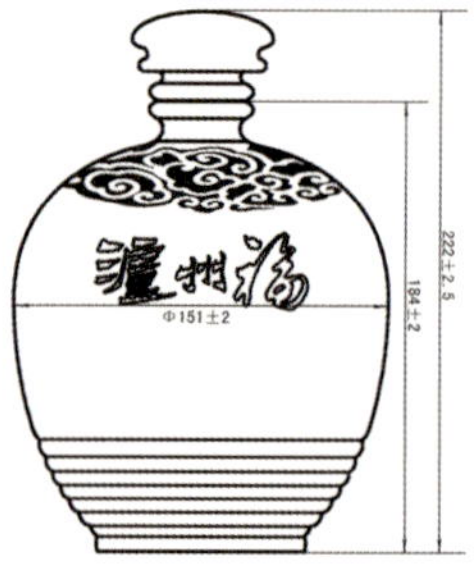

8．泸州福酒瓶

造型圆润敦实又不失细节，采用自由曲线构成的封闭式造型，以大弧线为主，配合瓶底层叠结构，使外轮廓弧线不再单调，在光线的照射下更显其造型的丰富层次变化。层叠结构增加手触摩擦力，使抓握酒瓶更加舒适安全，不易滑落。瓶盖同时也做了类似瓶底的结构，上下呼应，使酒瓶整体更为协调。瓶肩上装饰有传统祥云图案，若隐若现、起伏变化，含蓄内敛地表达着吉祥如意的美好愿望。配合经典的中国红，使其更具古老东方神韵。烫金的标志与文字将其十年典藏的品质展现无疑。

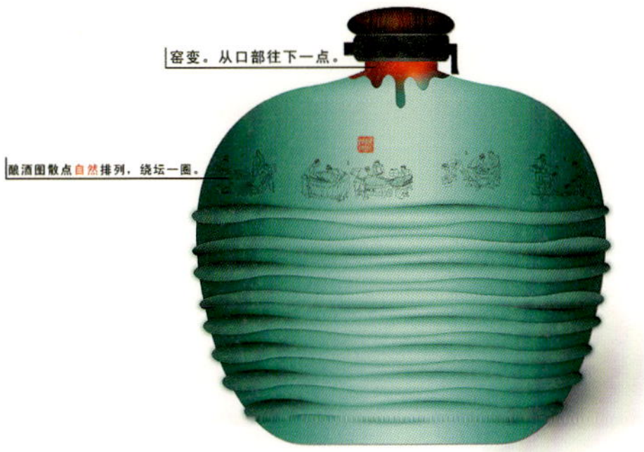

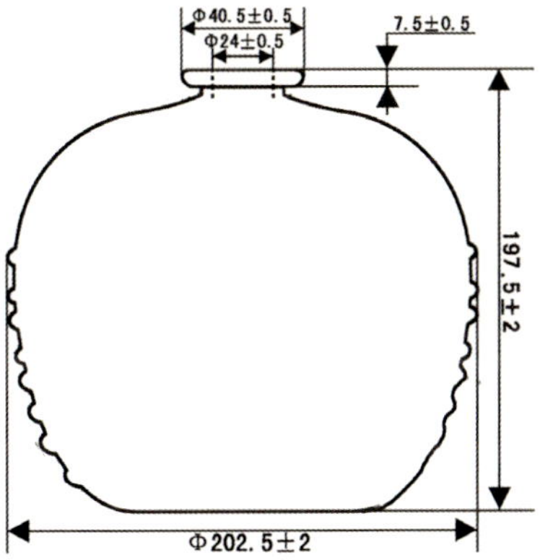

9．国窖1573

一坛好酒一个故事。使用坛子的传统造型，瓶颈部的曲线与下部的螺旋纹形成动静对比的生动形象，给人一种流动的感觉。瓶身大部分的波纹状起伏是使用麻绳捆绑过的痕迹，体现出偶发的美感特征。瓶身的青瓷质感给人一种历史文化悠久之感。瓶颈处有窑变出现的花纹，这样就为简洁的瓶体制造出丝丝生动。瓶盖使用红色顶子与瓶身的青色形成呼应搭配，与前面的窑变共同形成视觉穿插。瓶体下部的波纹起伏也符合人手把握的要求。上下线条慢慢收口和凸凹的瓶颈造型可以方便开启。瓶体上部的四周自然排布着传统酿酒场景绘画，显示白酒文化的历史传承性，同时古老的绘画手法体现出久远的酒文化和深沉的历史幽思。

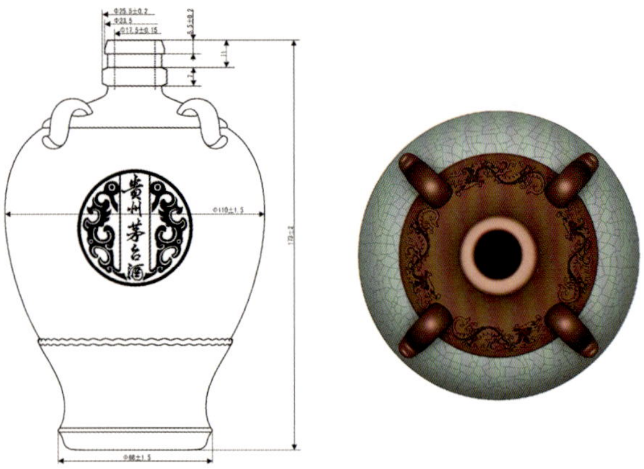

10．茅台

龙，王者的代表，茅台，酒中上品。

酒瓶配色古典大气，瓶体紫砂质感与裂纹釉不同质感的交替韵律出现，达到造型的和谐统一。瓶盖线条的变化与整个瓶身达成很好的默契，防滑条的设计、凹凸文字的装饰、颜色的变化无不体现出设计师的匠心独运，构思巧妙。瓶体一面运用中国龙纹图腾样式，另一面使用古典花纹和书法文字作为装饰，前后呼应。瓶颈处四个提耳连接着瓶肩与瓶身。瓶体底部使用竖向装饰线条，呈向上辐射之势，也是手托酒瓶时的实用考虑，这种线条变化不仅有上下呼应的作用也起到加固稳定瓶身的作用。

11．茅台——民间酒壶

酒壶造型新颖独特，以夸张的造型和不稳定的结构区别于传统酒瓶，突出酒瓶的实用价值。酒壶另辟蹊径，将酒杯与壶盖相互结合，酒杯在整体造型上既是充当壶盖角色，又可单独使用，增加了产品的附加价值，为自饮自酌提供方便。同时酒杯与酒壶皆以葫芦为原型进行仿生设计，做了收腰处理，文字构成的腰线优美流畅，两者在造型上高度统一，丝毫没有突兀之感。腰线位置指示出人手把握的角度，起到语意传达的作用。酒壶通体使用艳丽的红色，具有强烈的视觉冲击力，配合独特外形，更提升其独特的形式魅力。

12．舍得

舍与得，它凝聚东方智慧，体现出“禅”之意境。舍即是得，得即是舍。“舍”与“得”看似对立，实则统一，从大的范围看，舍得实际是一种人生哲理。这也正是此酒瓶采用两色黑白对比、色调又是和谐统一的造型语言之目的。

瓶体形状使用圆筒状，浑圆的体态没有多余的装饰，简简单单。表面使用紫砂具有细腻的手感，不做多余的装饰，让手在那种真实自然的表面中慢慢体会到平和。瓶颈处和瓶盖使用橘黄色和金色稍做装饰，在平淡中存在着华丽，平凡中品味美好的人生。正面使用中国书法中规中矩，将酒品的平淡内敛作了完美的诠释。

中华老字号

宜兴金鱼紫砂陶瓷酒瓶烧造技艺·造型设计个案分析

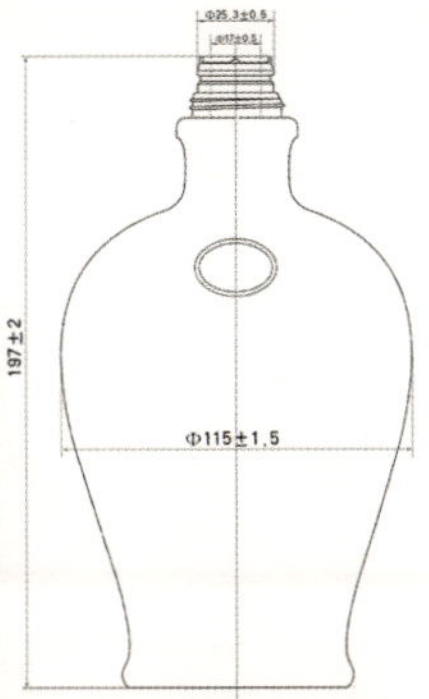

13．元曲

外形精致，花纹装饰具有精致的构成美感，整体隐约融入了秦汉漆器的设计元素。华丽却不失丰富的内涵，表面处理具有翡翠的晶莹剔透感。瓶体曲线柔美圆润，使用红色和金色的颜色搭配，高贵大方，从表面那种透明感中几乎可以感觉到里面流动的美酒。装饰花纹使用中国传统花卉纹样图案，寓意富贵吉祥。瓶颈和瓶口完整统一没有多余装饰，突出瓶身饱满造型。瓶盖略扁，与瓶身产生造型对比，有利于人的操作习惯。

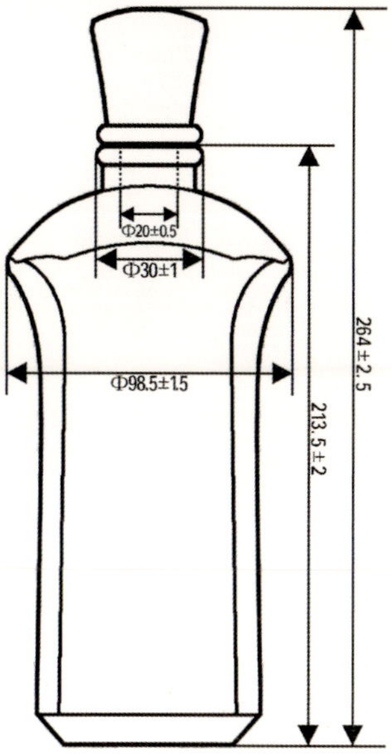

14．西凤兵马俑紫砂瓶

提炼秦兵马俑的造型元素为设计所用，形式抽象简洁，彰显出霸气威武之气。颜色使用灰色和黑色相互搭配，局部地方使用黄铜色，烘托出那种出自泥土的古韵，增加产品的档次和文化内涵。宽阔的肩膀、外翘挺拔的身体，瓶盖头部使用兵马俑的发簪与头冠的精练造型，形象生动传神。瓶体由下向上渐宽翻边的造型是考虑有利于手部抓取，形象上体现男子强壮的体态特征。图案的装饰采用古时官袍的前裙摆纹样，运用秦时的绘画手法，配合整体造型风格，凸显酒器神秘的色彩。

15．西凤——秦沣

暗红色彩釉的酒瓶中透出来自遥远古代的风韵，酒瓶以最为传统的酒壶造型为原型，壶肩处雕琢有祥云的凸纹，与光滑的瓶体形成质感上的对比，富于变化，瓶中央的圆形叠嵌在祥云图案之内，起到视觉中心的作用。瓶颈两边设计有提耳，过去人们将绳穿过壶耳，方便携带酒壶，设计中保留此造型是为了增加人们对酒瓶的认同感、亲切感。瓶体上印有金文和彩凤图案，大大增添了酒瓶的中国传统文化韵味。

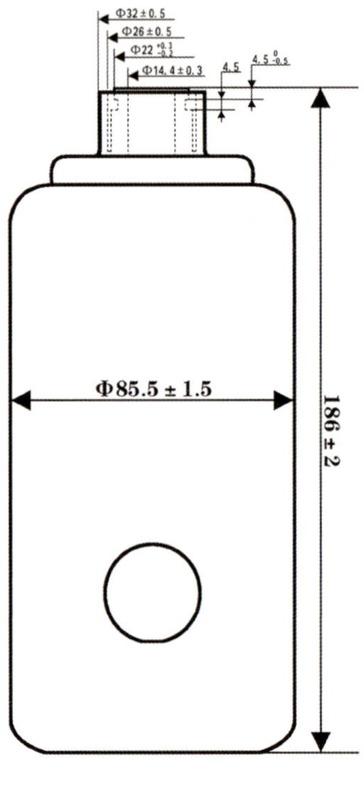

中华老字号

宜兴金鱼紫砂陶瓷酒瓶烧造技艺·造型设计个案分析

16．西凤——金鱼瓶

一款朴实无华的酒瓶设计，乍看之下并不起眼，细细品味却回味无穷。整体造型呈圆柱体，不加雕琢，瓶体与瓶盖比例适度。酒瓶如君子般内敛，却又散发出刚正不阿的气质。在瓶体圆柱体外轮廓线上设计有微妙的波纹起伏线条，使其如同手工制作而成，不加打磨，保持了最朴实的自然状态。同时波浪纹也起到增大摩擦力的作用，为酒瓶增加了良好的手感。而瓶颈处进行了阶梯状设计，为酒瓶的造型带来了丰富的变化。渐变的彩釉为酒瓶带来灵动的变化，似美酒在瓶中慢慢韵染。

中华老字号

宜兴金鱼紫砂陶瓷酒瓶烧造技艺·造型设计个案分析

17．西凤——凤型

此造型设计以仿生手法，对象征吉祥高贵的凤之形象加以提炼和简化，与酒瓶的功能相融合，巧妙的造型设计使两者的结合如此流畅自然。瓶盖的造型被设计成最为具象的凤首，设计精巧，凤首昂头向上，高歌吟唱，给予人们无限遐想。而瓶体却将凤的形象加以抽象，隐喻的设计神似凤尾凤翅，与瓶盖形成虚实对比，使造型更耐人寻味。设计者将凤尾的弧线设计成瓶把手，食指可穿孔而过，与瓶体紧密地连接在一起，强化了造型功能的可操作性。酒瓶整体使用原色的紫砂材质，温润低调、深沉内敛，再加上暗金色的花纹更显其低调的华丽。久久品味才能体味其优雅的气质。

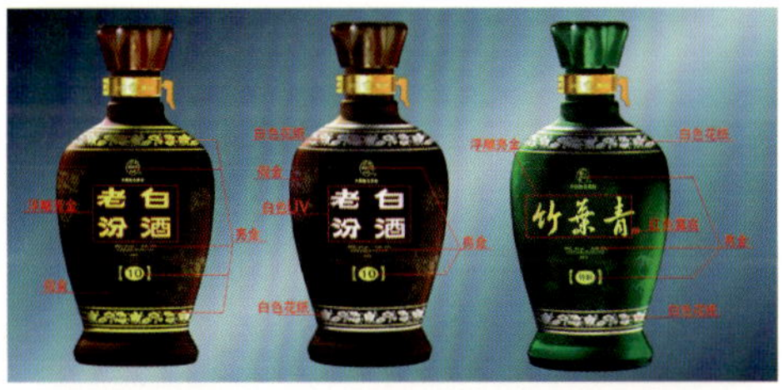

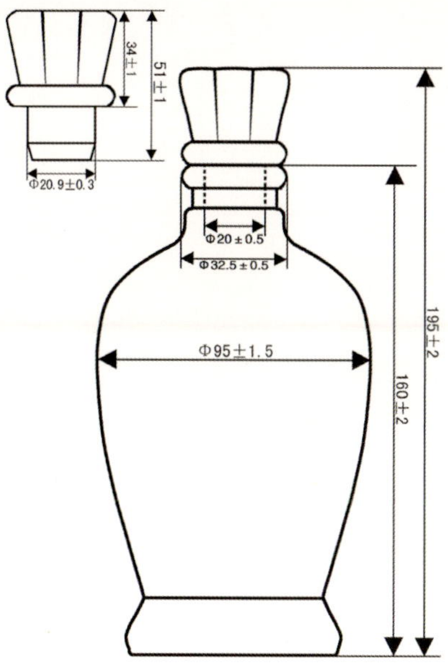

18．杏花村汾酒酒瓶

酒瓶造型朴实无华，摒弃了繁琐的线条，以最简洁的曲线延展变化描绘出酒瓶清晰大气的外轮廓，不加修饰，但却自然天成。瓶的底足是向外翻转的曲线，从功能上加大了底足的支撑面积，增强了瓶身的稳定性。酒瓶足部与瓶肩造型向内收拢，强化了造型形式的对比，使瓶体中部向外扩张的曲面更为饱满充实。壶盖与壶口链接处进行包边处理，与壶体的大曲线形成对比，虚实相生，丰富了酒瓶外轮廓线的多变性。壶盖采用自由曲面造型，像是罗绮轻轻盖在酒瓶上，又更像是古代君子的头冠，体现出酒、酒瓶与文化名人的悠久联系。在深色的酒瓶上装饰了两条金色的传统花瓣纹样，与瓶体造型共同营造出朴实的古韵气氛。

烧造技艺

❶ 二十世纪宜兴龙窑

一、宜兴陶瓷酒器传统烧造技艺

（一）工具及原料

1．工具

（1）矩车

用硬木制成的典型工具是矩车和木转盘，“没有规矩，不成方圆”，矩车用于划割壶底、盖片，稍有扭曲变形，切割出的壶盖和壶底就不圆，影响壶的外形和使用。

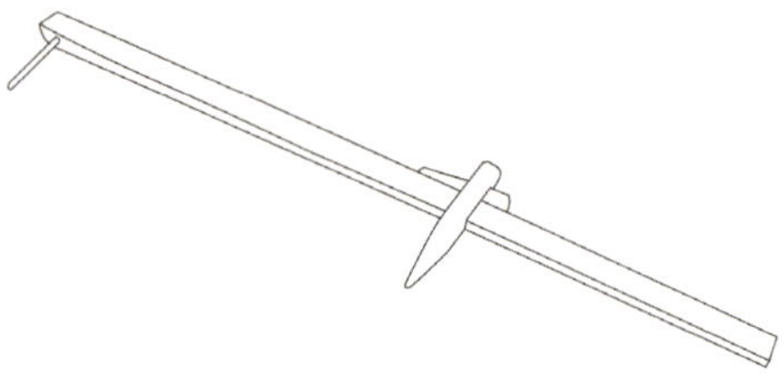

（2）木转盘

制作壶身的一个必备工具，转动成型之用。

（3）牛角制成的“明针”和“线梗”

各种“明针”和“线梗”，是用来光坯和规整壶身线条的最佳工具。（“光坯”是指使壶面细密光润的工序。也是制壶的最后一道工序，难度很大，要求反复刮磨，才能将表面的较大颗粒压进去，同时又把泥料中的泥浆刮出，形成润泽饱满的外形。）

中华老字号

宜兴陶瓷酒器传统烧造技艺·工具

牛角削薄做成的明针，在使用时要先浸泡，泡软后才能使用。把牛角片浸泡在水中，主要求其易弯而柔韧。但长期浸泡和使用后，明针就会腐烂和开裂，特别是在夏季和梅雨季节，这就要经常修剪明针的长短和弧度。

线梗是用来规整壶身线条的，艺人在做壶之前，要根据自己要做的壶形，制作出角度弧度合适的线梗。此外，线梗还用来光整壶身各个部位相互衔接的部位，使其光洁度和细密性保持一致。

牛角作为精加工的必要工具，主要是反复刮磨坯体，将表面的粗大颗粒压进坯体，使泥浆浮出，从而形成一细腻的表层，让坯体表面温润明鉴。

（4）皮磨布

在制壶过程中用到一种磨布，这种磨布可用牛羊皮，以柔软细腻的羊皮为最佳，主要用来光磨成型初期的棱角细节。

牛羊皮的表面有分布均匀的毛孔空隙，可以吸收壶坯中的水分，又不粘连泥料。另外，除了表面的纹理特征，牛羊皮还含有蛋白质和纤维，具有柔软细腻，弹力较大的特征。因此除了可以光坯，还可以裹在工具上整理细部。经其修整后的紫砂壶，可以避免过于光鲜亮丽的效果，产生一种质朴拙雅的质感。

（5）搭子

搭子是成型中的主要工具之一，主要用于打泥条，片子和捶嘴，把泥片等等。搭子的主要用材是榉树、檀树、枣树等，取材要干。搭子平时使用后用湿布擦净放在干燥处，不能在太阳下晒，不能用来打铁器等硬物。

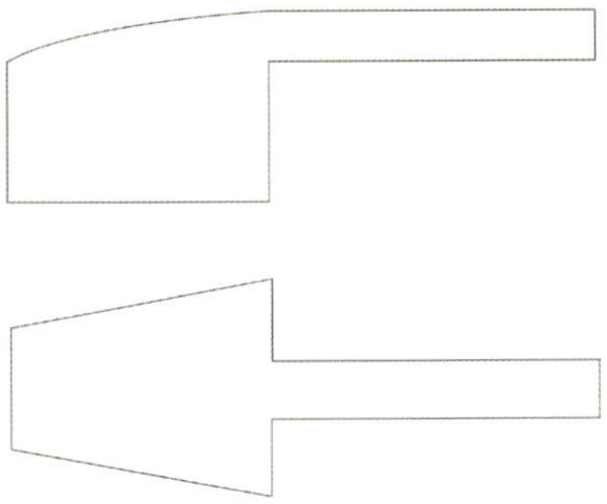

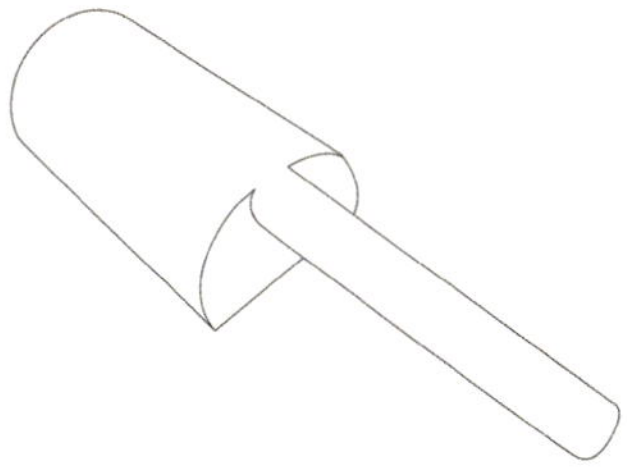

（6）竹拍子、刀

拍子主要用于打身筒，拍片子，拍口。材料以红木为最佳，拍子的总长28cm，拍身宽10cm。厚度是根据材质而定，枣木前厚3mm，中厚4mm，后厚4mm，柏木厚些，红木可更薄一些，拍子用过后也不能浸在水里，应放干燥处，要避免单面受潮，并要防止拍子开裂。

刀是成型中使用最广的工具，在制作过程中，用刀进行切、削、钎、挑、挟、挖、刮等，从开始到结束都要使用。金属工具主要使用铁、钢、铜三种材料加工。金属制刀具分鳑鲏刀和尖刀两种。

刀主要用来切削、平整、挖盖、潦坯、切泥等用，有大小、厚薄、利钝、长短之分，一般要用7～10把。尖刀要求的数量更多，主要用来贴花、通嘴、啄嘴、纹饰造型等。因制作大小、器形不同来选择合适的尖刀。

一般木质和竹制的尖刀用来修毛坯和整理大轮廓，金属制刀具用来切割和加工一次成型的工序，求其尖锐锋利、不拖泥带水的特征。金属类的刀具一般是由锻工先打制出毛坯，再由艺人根据自己需要，精心磨制加工后才能使用。

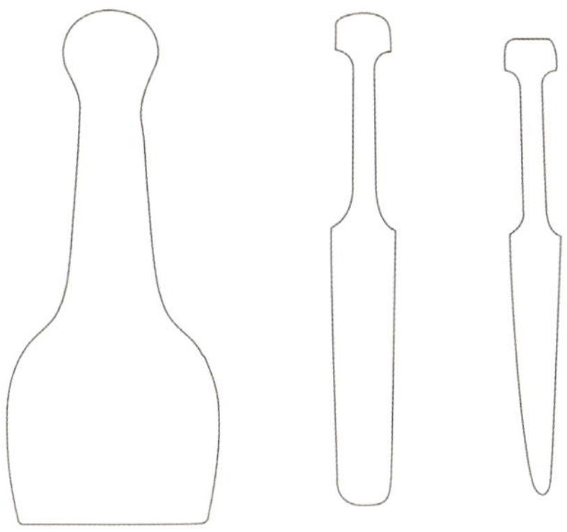

（7）木拍子

（8）用紫砂自制的工具

紫砂喷水壶是学徒要做的第一件紫砂作品，也是最典型的自制工具之一。

在做壶艺人中流传这样一个口诀："三分工，七分凉"，这是指在制成一把紫砂壶近半个月的时间里，如何使壶坯保持均衡不变的湿度，是制作成功的关键因素。喷水壶就成为必备工具之一，传统喷水壶一般体积较小，壶上有个横置的小管，管口下部的壶盖上有个小洞，用嘴对着小管吹气，就可根据虹吸原理将水从小洞喷出。有意思的是，用嘴吹气时，不能用力太大，要轻轻的才能将水吹出均匀的雾化效果。

（9）花板（花饰模具）

是艺人自己用紫砂制成的工具。一般是由做好母模后，再用紫砂泥料翻模烧制而成的。这种模具制出的花饰多放在壶钮、壶盖上，题材大都是寓意吉祥的花卉、动物等，如：龙头、梅花、寿桃、竹子。每个紫砂壶艺人都有自己擅长的壶形和花饰，这些花饰模具，就是为了保证纹样一致整齐、风格稳定。

传统的花板（模具），艺人用紫砂泥料自制的花饰模具。

2．原料

中华老字号

宜兴陶瓷酒器传统烧造技艺·酒壶的生产工艺及流程

（二）宜兴传统酒壶烧造技艺流程

1．取料

（1）原料的准备，包括挖泥、炼泥和选料。矿中挖出的硬块状的泥料经过捣碎、过筛、澄滤，所得细土下窑储藏，称为“养土”。

（2）使用割弓切取适量的紫砂泥料

2．揉泥

在木案上进行反复揉压，使其具有韧性，便于拉坯成型。

3. 拉坯

(1) 造型

将泥放置在拉坯车上拉坯，拉制过程中加入适量的水。配合锯条在坯体表面刮制，使其表面光滑。根据酒壶造型与体积的不同，工具可随时调整。

（2）修整

用手敲击瓶子底部检查厚度，根据制作者的感觉与经验判断是否需要进一步修整。用手掌敲拍壶体检查是否对称，也是为了检查壶体横截面是否接近正圆。修壶体。

（3）工具

制好的坯要经过细致的修整，结合传统工具和自制工具进行形态塑造。

早期的制坯工具主要是一种竹刀，后来逐步增添了木、角、石、金属等质料的工具，并用陶轮来拉坯和修坯。到清代，工具有十多种，包括椎、碓、镖、钗，有圭形、笏形、贝形、肾形、月形、蝎尾形等多种形状。

4．制作壶盖

壶盖造型、切口沿。壶盖与壶口进行反复比对，检查是否匹配。使用调刀进行造型和倒圆。

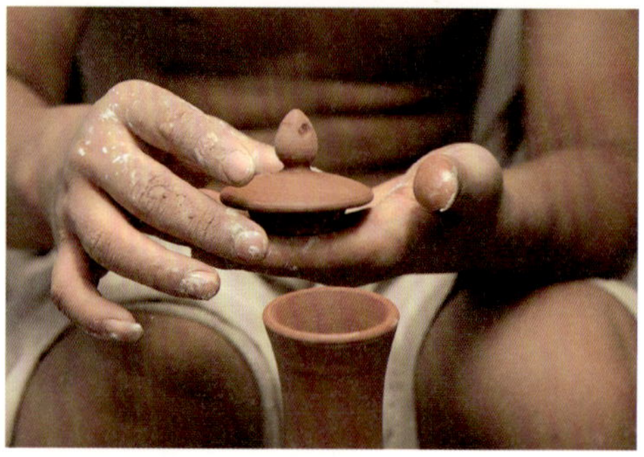

5．制作壶嘴、壶把

（1）做壶嘴

和泥、转动使其圆整。担一下是否水平和均匀。画记号，使用挖嘴刀（铜管或不锈钢管）通壶嘴。在壶身挖孔，根据大小挖小孔，一般为三排，中间孔多，两边渐少，此壶为13个孔。使用脂泥将壶嘴粘连在壶身上。

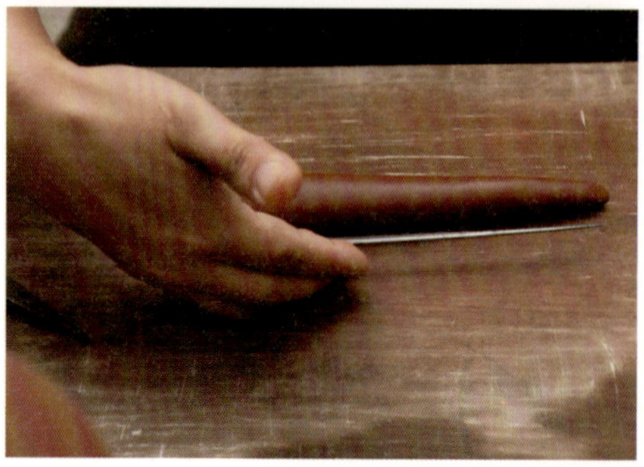

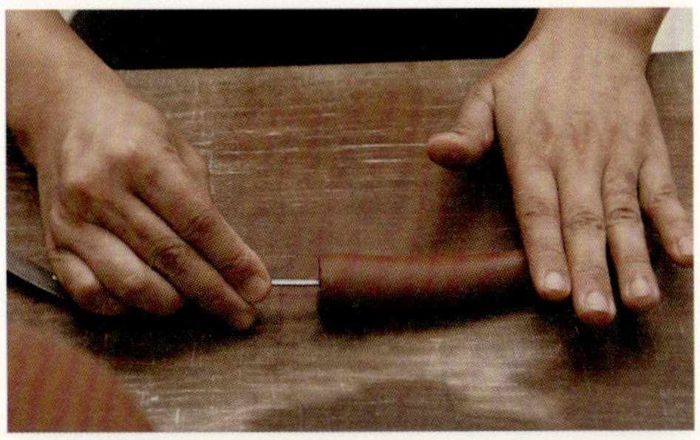

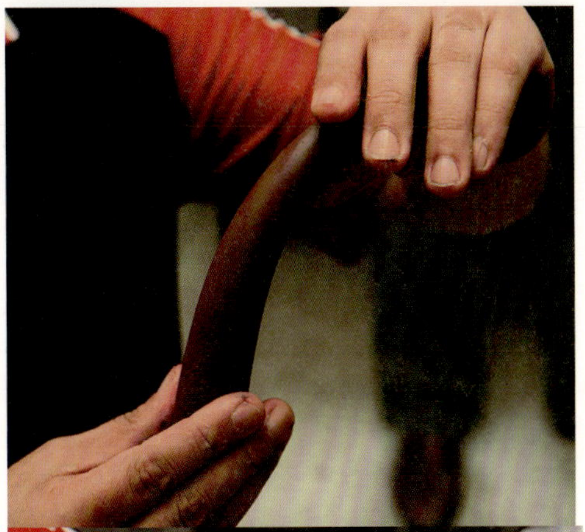

（2）做壶把

壶把的制作除不进行挖孔与通嘴外，其他与壶嘴制作过程相同。

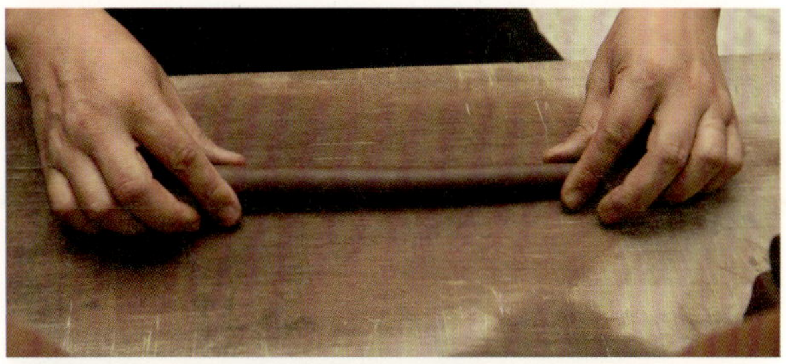

6．刮坯

刮坯之前坯体需要10个小时左右的干燥，放置室外干燥会快一点。用水笔将干燥后的坯体弄湿，使用板刀修壶口、壶脚和壶底部，对壶体表面进行细致修整。

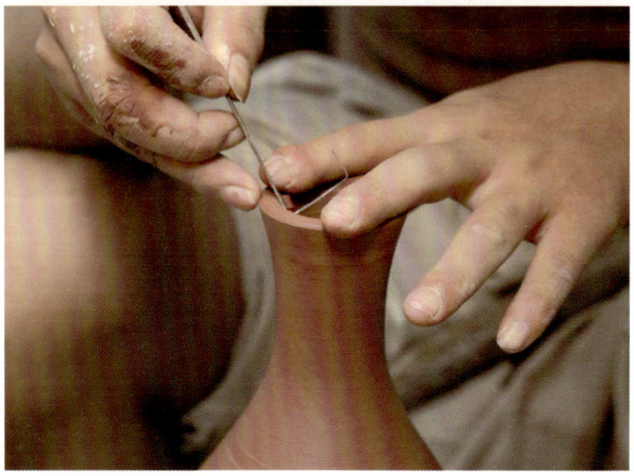

7．烧制

（三）宜兴传统酒坛烧造技艺流程

1. 炼泥（和泥）

反复捶泥成泥块，湿抹布覆盖，保持水分待用。

2. 做底

（1）开料

在泥凳上将含水量16%的泥块打成泥片，用矩车按照所需尺寸划成圆形后，用竹括括空表面，翻底放置于板盘上。再根据酒坛尺寸取适量的泥块，再在泥凳上打泥片成长方形，用矩车按照所需弧度划成扇形。

宜兴陶瓷酒器传统烧造技艺·酒坛的生产工艺及流程

（2）围底

由两人托起扇形泥片，立起，围在板盘的圆形泥片四周，合起后除去多余泥片，用手将接缝处密死。

（3）做圆

手持木制拍子在外，里手捶在内拍打刚刚竖起泥片，两手要协调，使底越来越圆。

（4）做直

料角在外，手在内，向上刮，使底越来越挺直、饱满。

（5）料边

（6）喂泥

用水分较大的泥填充于所有泥片连接处，起到黏合的作用。

（7）光坯

用橡皮刮匀里外泥片，使其光滑细腻。

（8）找平补眼

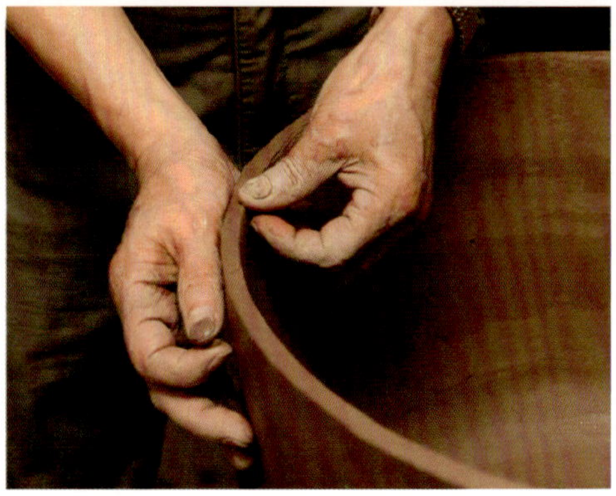

（9）干燥

（10）覆底

当干燥到一定程度，泥不粘手，有一定硬度，立得住时，将坛底翻过来。

（11）凹底

用里手捶在底部中央轻轻往下捶，干燥一会儿。

宜兴陶瓷酒器传统烧造技艺·酒坛的生产工艺及流程

3．做幔

4．做口

5．装窑

6．烧制

7．出窑

（四）宜兴传统酒缸烧造技艺流程

1．捶泥

它是成型的第一道工序。捶泥的目的是使泥质匀顺，水分分布均匀。方法是先将经过炼制的块状泥料放在工作台上，用木榔头反复捶炼，一般应捶炼三遍，这样可使泥质均匀细腻，黏性加强，便于制作；同时可以使泥坯减少缺陷。泥料捶炼后，划成泥条。

2．打泥片

取条状的熟泥数块，放在工作台上用搭子打成泥片。打泥片时手持木制的搭子，落下时必须端正着实，注意厚薄均匀，然后按照图纸要求尺寸，划成泥片。

3．做底

做底以前，先在木制内模上敷上一层干釉粉，便于模型脱出。做底时先取泥片长条围在模型四周，再以圆形泥片作为底片。底片应比木模底部周围大25厘米左右，用拍子将长出的部分与先围在模型上的泥条打紧接牢，然后脱出模型，再用含水量约23%的软泥在四周底角补满，同时用橡皮光一遍，使补上去的泥黏结牢固。

4．晒底

底部制成后，凡制大中型陶器，尚须另用泥条逐段加高缸身，称之为接缸筒。在接缸筒前，需先将底部晾晒。晒底的目的，是使底部坯体略加干燥硬化，在接缸筒时不致变形。在晒底时，以逐渐干燥为原则，一般均在室内阴干，如必须放在太阳光下晾晒，上面应覆盖草席。晒底到含水量15%左右时，放置室内，将缸底的上口着地，底部在上，用陶制的里手柱在底部中央轻敲，捶成凹形。捶底的目的，是使陶器在烧成时不致发生裂底的缺陷。如做平底产品，捶底这一工序就可省去。

5．接缸筒

将底坯周围用棒柱拍击打坚，打成光坯，使厚薄均匀，泥质坚实，然后进行接缸筒。将预先做成的泥圈接在底坯上口，接合时，把上下接头割成凹凸楔口，一般上段为凹，下段为凸。楔口割成，然后用羊毛排笔在接头处涂上适量的水，使泥质变软，再在接头内外涂抹一层胶泥（含水量25%～28%）进行黏结。接缝周围还须用软泥补足刮平，使接头牢固。这样逐段加高，接好缸筒。

6．制作缸口

缸筒干燥到一定程度，就可制作缸口。制缸口边沿的泥料，应细腻润熟，含水量20%左右。制作缸口时，将泥料握紧直接在缸筒上口捏制。沿口应制得饱满平整，然后用浸水粗布安放在沿口上，用大拇指卡紧，磨圆勒光几周即成。

7．整形

口沿做好后，坯件已初步成型。接着以木制棒柱和陶制里手柱在坯的里外相衬拍击整形，使坯质坚实。陶制的里手柱托在坯件内部，棒柱打击坯件外部。打紧后，再修整缸沿一次，阴干到整个坯件含水量5%～7%时，即可施釉。

8．上釉

9．晒干

10．装窑

11．烧制

12．出窑

宜兴陶瓷酒器传统烧造技艺·酒缸的生产工艺及流程

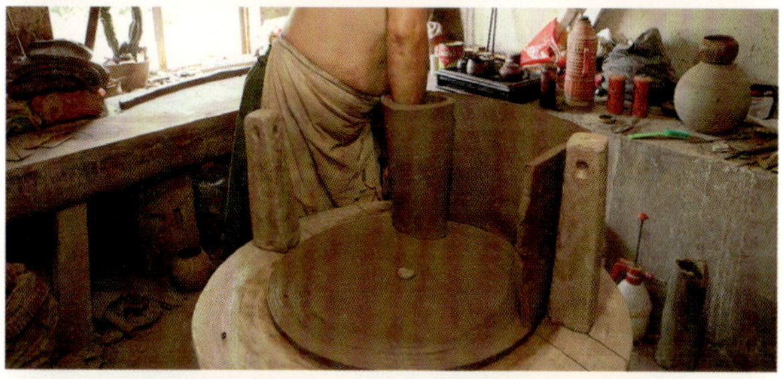

宜兴陶瓷酒器传统烧造技艺·酒缸的生产工艺及流程

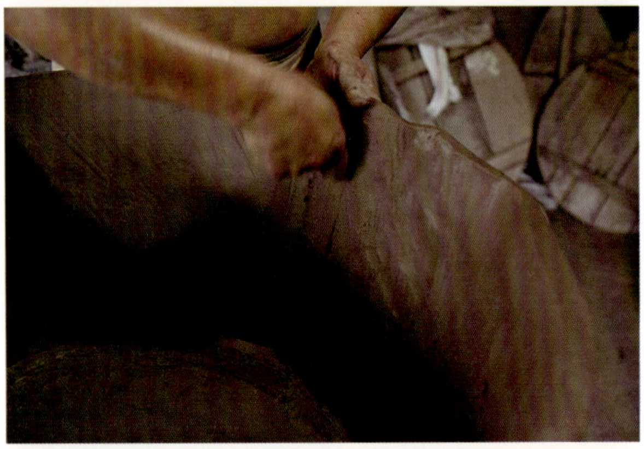

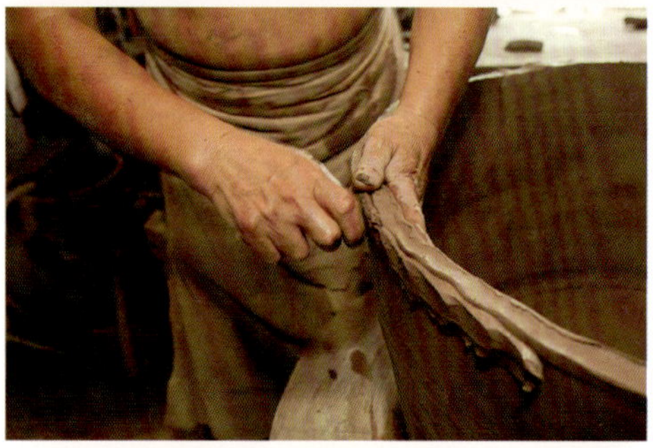

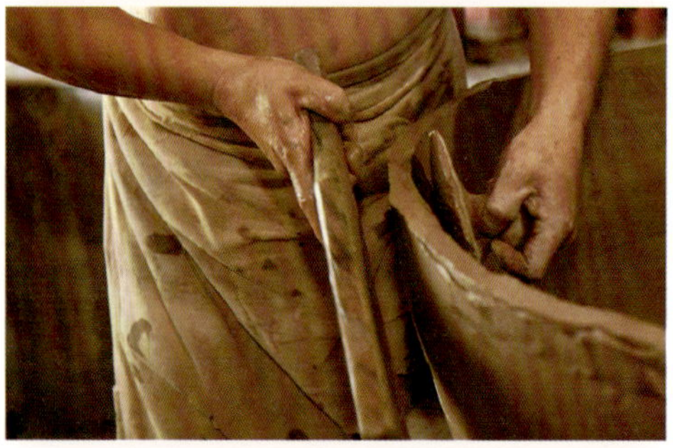

宜兴陶瓷酒器传统烧造技艺·酒缸的生产工艺及流程

二、宜兴金鱼紫砂陶瓷酒瓶烧造技艺

（一）原料与工具

1．原料

紫泥、段泥、红泥、夹泥

（二）生产工艺及流程

1．设计

2．打样

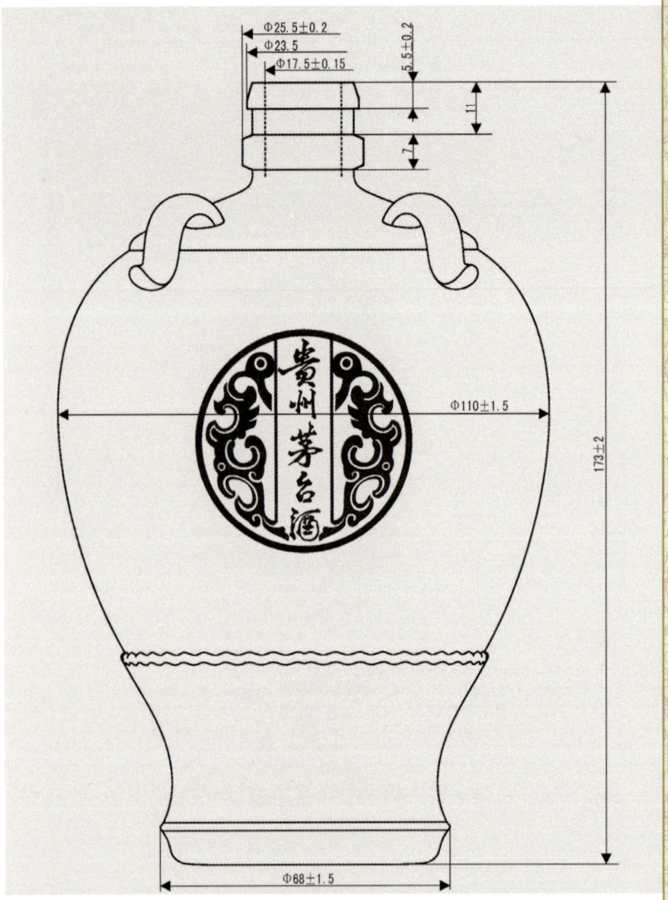

3．磨料

中华老字号

金鱼紫砂陶瓷酒瓶传统制作工艺流程

4．做种

3～6个模/10000个瓶子

5．翻模

做生产模具

6. 烘干模具

7. 灌浆

8. 回浆

9. 脱坯

中华老字号

金鱼紫砂陶瓷酒瓶传统制作工艺流程

10．阴干、干燥

11．插牙齿

12．去除模线

13．测量瓶口内径

14．磨头

15. 光坯

16. 控制牙齿

17. 清坯

18. 验坯

19. 瓶口打蜡

20. 内壁挂釉

21. 入窑烧制

22. 上蜡

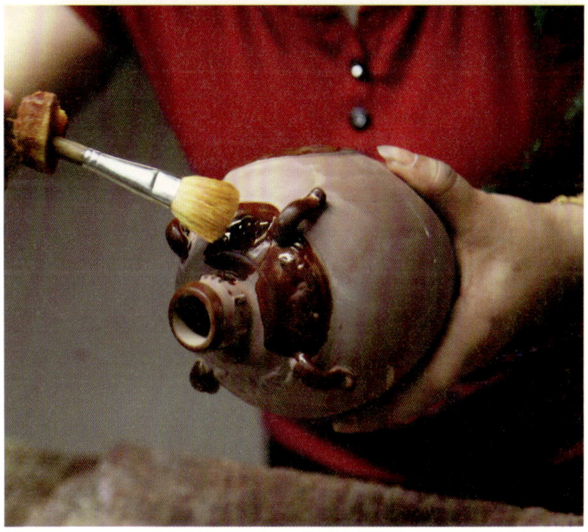

23. 外挂釉

24．二次烧制

25．二次上蜡

26．外挂釉

27．三次烧制

28．三次上蜡

29．外挂釉

30．四次烧制

31．做开片

32．贴花纸

33．五次烧制

（三）质量标准

1．紫砂陶瓷酒瓶的外形、容积、尺寸必须符合设计图样及技术文件的要求。

2．紫砂陶瓷酒瓶的吸水率应≤1.0%，无裂穿和渗漏现象。

3．紫砂陶瓷酒瓶内壁与酒接触面的铅、镉溶出量应符合GB14147－93《陶瓷包装容器铅、镉溶出量允许极限》的规定。

4．紫砂陶瓷酒瓶的外观质量必须符合设计要求，表面光洁光滑，无明显缺陷。

5．紫砂陶瓷酒瓶贴花烤花后，花标图案、文字清晰，无明显缺陷。

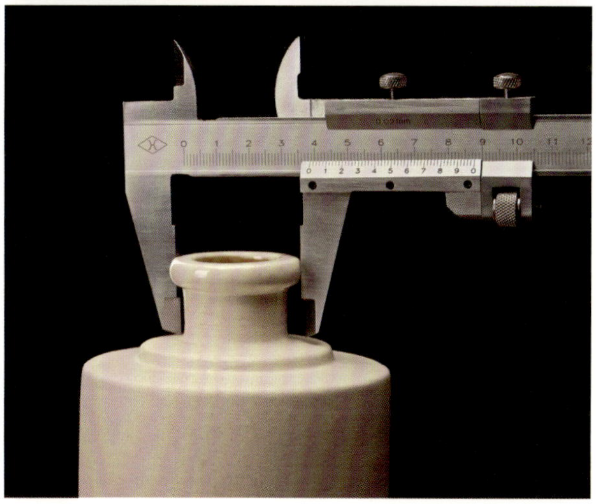

老字号与传承人

1 20世纪50年代的宜兴陶都老字号商业街

中华老字号

宜兴金鱼紫砂陶瓷酒瓶烧造技艺·店铺与销售

一、店铺与销售

（一）宜兴销售陶瓷酒器老字号店铺一览表

1. 1850—1911年间开设的老字号店铺

地点	店号	店主	开设时间
上海	鲍生泰	鲍家	1850年
上海	葛德和	葛德和	1860年
江苏 常熟 浒浦	诚泰	鲍家	1870年
浙江 常浦	同泰	鲍家	1875年
上海	福康	陈子环	1880年
江苏 常熟 浒浦	陈义隆	陈子环	1880年
江苏 江阴	元隆盛	陈子环	1880年
杭州	张万清	张自清	1903年
常州	永大昌	鲍家	1910年
无锡	信泰	鲍家	1910年
无锡	鲍金泰	鲍家	1910年

2.1912—1924年间开设的老字号店铺

地点	店号	店主	开设时间
上海	鲍源信	鲍家	约1912—1924年
上海	谊大新	不详	约1912—1924年
上海	铁画轩	不详	约1912—1924年
上海	吴德盛	陈子环	约1912—1924年
上海	章新泰	鲍家	约1912—1924年
上海	利用	不详	约1912—1924年
上海	兴盛栈	不详	约1912—1924年
杭州	源隆顺	不详	约1912—1924年
杭州	兴昌	不详	约1912—1924年
天津	豫丰	不详	约1912—1924年
烟台	同品祥	不详	约1912—1924年
青岛	和盛	陈子环	约1912—1924年
武汉	不详	不详	约1912—1924年
无锡	蒋义茂	不详	约1912—1924年
无锡	蒋仁茂	不详	约1912—1924年
常州	永泰	鲍家	约1912—1924年
南通	瑞泰	鲍家	约1912—1924年
南通	盛泰	鲍家	约1912—1924年
镇江	鲍信盛	鲍家	约1912—1924年

（二）宜兴生产日用陶瓷、酒器企业一览表

1．1956—1988年宜兴生产缸器企业

单　　位	产　品	型　号　规　格	年　产　量	备　　注
大新陶瓷厂	缸　器	定制　特制　普通	合计20万件左右	1990年后，淘汰部分滞销缸器，将普通5号大缸口径、体形加大使之与容量600千克定制缸配套，同时将普通1号大缸的容量增至500千克，维持少量生产
建筑陶瓷厂	缸　器	定制　特制　普通		
均陶工艺厂	缸　器	定制　特制　普通		
红旗陶瓷厂	缸　器	定制　特制　普通		
东风陶瓷厂	缸　器	定制　特制　普通		
正新陶瓷厂	缸　器	定制　特制　普通		

2．1988—1992年宜兴生产酒坛企业

单　　位	产　品	容　量　规　格	年　产　量	备　　注
大新陶瓷厂	酒　坛	350千克～500千克	15万件	大新、建筑、均陶陶瓷厂三个企业烧造容量350千克～500千克酒坛
建筑陶瓷厂	酒　坛	350千克～500千克	15万件	
均陶工艺厂	酒　坛	350千克～500千克	15万件	
建新陶瓷厂	酒　坛	5千克～180千克	15万件	建新、正新、胜利、红旗、东风陶瓷厂五个企业烧造容量5千克～180千克酒坛
正新陶瓷厂	酒　坛	5千克～180千克	15万件	
胜利陶瓷厂	酒　坛	5千克～180千克	15万件	
红旗陶瓷厂	酒　坛	5千克～180千克	15万件	
东风陶瓷厂	酒　坛	5千克～180千克	15万件	
宜兴非金属化工机械厂	工业陶酒坛	5千克～180千克	1.8万件	1994年该厂与丁蜀镇任墅村合资，创办宜兴市宇盛化工陶瓷厂
宜兴市宇盛化工陶瓷厂	酒　坛	5千克～180千克		

3．1992—2005年宜兴生产酒瓶企业

单　　位	产　品	品　　牌	年产量	备　　注
宜兴青瓷厂	酒　瓶	1994年成功研制具有防伪作用的高档釉面螺纹口酒瓶	2000多万件	容水量：750、500、250、125毫升4种1992—1993年生产传统酒瓶
金鱼陶瓷有限公司	酒　瓶	“金鱼牌”陶瓷酒瓶获江苏省名牌产品	2005年产量合计6000多万件	
宜兴彩陶工艺厂	酒　瓶	“艺萃牌”陶瓷酒瓶获无锡市名牌产品		
暗星陶瓷有限公司	酒　瓶	不　　详		

4．宜兴生产酒瓶企业档案

字　号	创立时间	创立人	现任掌柜	从业技工	坐落位置	备　　注
宜兴金帆陶瓷	1992年5月	谈志坚	谈珂	1500多名	宜兴市丁蜀镇南环路3	荣获“全国外商投资‘双优’企业”、“无锡市‘三信’企业”、“宜兴市明星企业”、“宜兴市开放型经济先进集体”、“丁蜀镇文明企业”、“丁蜀镇工业应税销售、自营出口外汇、劳动和社会保障先进单位”等荣誉称号

字　号	创立时间	创立人	现任掌柜	从业技工	坐落位置	备　注
昊源陶瓷		宜兴梅青陶瓷有限公司以及昊源陶瓷开发中心组成			宜兴市丁蜀镇汤蜀东路二号	
宜兴彩陶工艺厂	20世纪50～60年代		葛柏初	拥有工艺大师在内的各类技艺人员80多名	宜兴市丁蜀镇公园路西口	多次荣获全国陶瓷评比金奖、江苏省新产品金奖、无锡市名牌产品、无锡市知名商标等奖项
玉阳陶瓷			杨岳军		宜兴市湖㳇镇金桥组	
易人陶瓷	20世纪90年代		钱钢	100余名	宜兴市丁蜀镇塍里村丁蜀镇轻工业学校对面	祖法制陶
宜兴市青瓷陶艺厂				70余人	宜兴市丁蜀镇边庄村边庄路	陶都五朵金花之一 2007年1月
宜兴青瓷厂		崔鹤鸣			宜兴丁蜀镇	1998年12月
碧玉青瓷有限公司					丁蜀镇边庄	“碧玉青瓷”文字印章款式为注册商标2007年
中远青瓷厂	1999年				宜兴市丁蜀镇通蜀村	代表作有“狮虎挂盘”、“青瓷碑瓶”、“剑气”、“古盆钵”、“水注系列”、“纹片青瓷组合”等

（三）销售区域分布

1．1912—1924年全国陶瓷器出口量价值表

年　代	出口海关量	年　代	出口海关量
1912	908639	1919	752757
1913	986002	1920	700507
1914	862445	1921	666311
1915	830152	1922	648045
1916	1092081	1923	951666
1917	942351	1924	1202892
1918	678790		

2．1924—1937年全国陶瓷器出口量价值表

年　　代	出口海关量	年　　代	出口海关量
1924	1202892	1931	765754
1925	769584	1932	390279
1926	850193	1933	385587
1927	882828	1934	370528
1928	848424	1935	459769
1929	679085	1936	515929
1930	778961	1937	354258

据不完全统计，截至目前，金帆旗下的金鱼酒瓶已与下列高档酒厂商开展了密切的合作，取得了丰硕的成果。这些高档酒厂商分别为：

贵州茅台酒厂有限责任公司

1998年开始合作至今，产品涉及18种款式，生产酒瓶共计350万只。

五粮液集团有限公司

2005年开始合作至今，产品涉及5个系列21种款式，生产酒瓶共计180万只。

安徽口子酒业股份有限公司

至今为止已合作13年，产品涉及8个系列39种款式，生产酒瓶共计300万只。

酒鬼酒股份有限公司

2005年开始合作至今，产品涉及4个系列12种款式，生产酒瓶共计160万只。

山西杏花村汾酒集团有限责任公司

2005年开始合作至今，产品涉及3个系列8种款式，生产酒瓶共计260万只。

四川郎酒集团有限责任公司

2006年开始合作至今，产品涉及4个系列14种款式，生产酒瓶共计106万只。

泸州老窖集团有限责任公司

2006年开始合作至今，产品涉及45种款式，生产酒瓶共计400万只。

陕西西凤酒股份有限公司

2007年开始合作至今，产品涉及5个系列19种款式，生产酒瓶共计110万只。

二、传承有序的代表性“老字号”与掌门人

（一）老字号变迁

地　　点	变更名称	负责人	时　　间
宜　　兴	泥龙头生产作坊		1922年—1956年1月
宜　　兴	鹤鸣陶瓷厂	崔鹤鸣	1956年1月—1958年4月
宜　　兴	宜兴耐火电瓷厂		1958年4月—1960年
宜　　兴	宜兴电瓷厂		1960年—1966年
宜　　兴	宜兴金帆陶瓷有限公司	谈志坚	1992年5月至今
宜　　兴	宜兴金鱼草陶瓷有限公司	谈志坚	1992年5月—1997年4月
宜　　兴	宜兴金鱼陶瓷厂	谈志坚	1997年4月—2003年10月
宜　　兴	宜兴市金鱼陶瓷有限公司	谈　轲	2003年10月至今

（二）宜兴金鱼紫砂陶瓷酒瓶烧造技艺传承人、掌门人谈志坚

“学用结合，延展至今，其卓越成就始终屹立不移。”

谈志坚，江苏宜兴人士，生于新中国第一个五年计划期间的1954年。带着强烈理想主义情结的他在年轻时，一直希望能将社会成就和个人成就融合起来。谈志坚出身于干部家庭，自小耳濡目染官场的风雨变幻，却不为所动，而是把自己交给了陶瓷事业。

五六十年代军歌嘹亮，红色是这代人最深刻的记忆，他们都有着一股不可磨灭的英雄主义情结。童年时代，聪慧的谈志坚是玩伴们的领袖，心中早早埋下了一颗不为人后、永不服输的种子。童年的眼神里隐藏着命运的走向，漫长的人生皆是童年的延伸。1971年谈志坚初中毕业后未能进入更高学府学习深造，而是进入了当地的宜兴青瓷厂，做了一名普通技术工人，从此与陶瓷结下了不解之缘，踏上了攀登陶瓷巅峰的漫漫长路。

青瓷在宜兴有着上千年的悠久历史，宜兴青瓷厂成立于20世纪五六十年代，由江苏省轻工厅、宜兴县政府和陶瓷业界按照周总理的指示精神共同努力创办。1961年开始复烧青瓷计划，1963年试制成功，1965年开始出口，至1966年该厂青瓷已发展到200多个品种，产品以日用品和装饰艺术品为主。谈志坚在宜兴青瓷厂做了五年技术工人。他进厂最初做车工，车工的工作比较简单，是青瓷厂最底层的工种。

虽然生长在陶都，但在青瓷厂车间的工作是谈志坚第一次近距离真切地接触陶瓷，一坨泥土在师傅们的手中变幻出各种造型，经过一道道精细工序，变成一个个鲜活、典雅又充满灵性的陶器，谈志坚被深深地吸引了。此时青瓷技艺的传承仍是传统的师傅带徒弟式的手口相传，五年间他辗转于青瓷生产的各个车间，边干边学，细致观察琢磨工作的每一个细节，不断向老师傅讨教。老师傅们也都喜欢这个踏实肯干肯学的小伙子，对他的问题向来问一答十。谈志坚也不孚众望，往往能做到举一反三，令传授者深感欣慰。对陶瓷和陶瓷生产了解得越多，越能感到自身的不足，在不停地钻研学习中谈志坚总梦想着可以进入专门的学府学到更多的知识，以弥补自身理论知识的欠缺和不足。功夫不负有心人，凭着已经熟练掌握的高中课程和多年的陶瓷生产实践经验，谈志坚顺利通过了高考，然而，造化弄人，录取他

中华老字号

宜兴金鱼紫砂陶瓷酒瓶烧造技艺·老字号掌门人谈志坚

①掌门人谈志坚近影

掌门人档案
谈志坚
中华老字号宜兴金鱼紫砂陶瓷酒瓶烧造技艺传承人、掌门人
宜兴市金鱼陶瓷有限公司董事长

中华老字号

宜兴金鱼紫砂陶瓷酒瓶烧造技艺·老字号掌门人谈志坚

的学校并不是他报考的那所机械学校，而是南京化工学院（现为南京工业大学）的陶瓷专业。大学期间，谈志坚主要进修陶瓷机械、陶瓷工艺、陶瓷窑炉热工等专业课程。忆起这段经历，谈志坚笑言，这是老天的安排。

学成归来，鉴于谈志坚五年的基层工作经验和三年的理论学习，领导把他被分配到了江苏省宜兴陶瓷公司机动处，担任技术员。期间，谈志坚发挥本身优势以过硬的技术和极强的创新能力，赢得了公司领导的一致好评。1980年2月，谈志坚被调至宜兴青瓷厂技术科，担任副科长，负责青瓷技术工作。熟悉的厂房、熟悉的机器、熟悉的人，谈志坚的创造激情热烈的燃起。历经一年时间，谈志坚的技术研究顺利通过生产实践检验，他的技术理念也为大家折服，他个人也因此成为了厂里最年轻的技术专家。

自古鞭打快马，1982年国家轻工业部下达了《54米青瓷节能隧道窑》的设计制造项目，厂里研究决定将这个任务交给谈志坚，由他全权负责。谈志坚不负众望，带领团队废寝忘食，苦心钻研，仅一年时间，就完成了项目攻坚。在国家权威部门的检验下，该项目一次性通过了节能、技术等环节的验收，很快投产使用，成为当时国内能耗低、技术最先进的青瓷生产窑炉。这件事很快传遍国内陶瓷界，宜兴青瓷厂出名了，谈志坚也因此得到了业界知名专家的肯定，在陶瓷界牢牢地站稳了脚跟。

大家惊叹，谈志坚是陶瓷界的奇才！十多年浸染于陶瓷界，谈志坚却并未被陶瓷界固有的传统生产方式和思维方式所束缚，相反，他更加的清醒，清楚在关键时刻他需要什么，该去哪里寻找。在博大精深的民族本土文化艺术中，谈志坚汲取多种文化元素与艺术营养，不断探索青瓷材质的运用、青瓷釉料的配方、高温窑炉内的化学变化以及由此变幻出的色泽及审美意义，掌握了其内在的规律，并不停地以严谨、科学的方法去创新青瓷艺术。1986年，谈志坚负责并参与研制成功了省列"青瓷成套餐具"项目，获得了江苏省科技成果二等奖。这种高档成套青瓷艺术餐具，作为唯一的国产餐具进入了中国首家五星级酒店上海静安希尔顿酒店。

1988年8月谈志坚升任宜兴青瓷厂厂长，在厂长任期的4年间，宜兴青瓷生产进一步繁荣壮大，青瓷产品拓展至1000多个品种。宜兴青瓷厂经过30年的奋斗、30年的传承发展，其青中泛蓝的宜兴青瓷一举成为宜兴产区的精华，赢得了"东方蓝宝石、精美碧玉器"的美称，成为国家传统工艺保护产品，并被外交部、文化部列为国家定点礼品生产企业，其产品曾多次被作为国礼赠送给外国元首。对于青瓷，谈志坚有着发自肺腑的感情与体悟："陶瓷让我感受到人类历史的悠远，更令我时时不忘中国曾经拥有的经济辉煌与文化灿烂。身在宜兴，我与青瓷特有着魂牵梦萦的不解之缘。"

1

①2008年5月谈志坚与韩美林、瞿根年在北京
③1998年8月谈志坚赴英国考察陶瓷印花设备
④1999年谈志坚在英国考察
②⑤⑥谈志坚在宜兴金鱼紫砂陶瓷酒瓶烧造技艺研讨会及田野考察工作现场

担任国企厂长期间，谈志坚有着自己的一套独特管理模式。为了让管理更加高效便捷，他建立了一系列逻辑严密、运转科学的管理系统，当上级要求他设立副厂长时，他一口回绝，理由是不需要。之后企业发展所取得的一个个成就证明了谈志坚管理模式的成功，体现了他高超的领导能力和管理艺术。

1992年，受邓小平南巡讲话的鼓舞，谈志坚信心百倍，酝酿着一系列新的改革计划，准备将青瓷厂推向更高辉煌。然而，上天却在此时与谈志坚开了一个天大的玩笑，他被调离了青瓷厂，组织安排其前往宜兴环保工业园做副总经理，工业园是市级单位，由市长兼任总经理。这是个既风光又清闲的好差事。但离开了陶瓷，少了忙碌的谈志坚，从上班第一天开始就失落了。

到新单位上任不满一周，谈志坚就提出了辞职。1993年5月，他又拒绝了广东陶瓷协会会长的邀请，留在了当地，担任起村办企业“金鱼草陶瓷有限公司（后更名为金鱼陶瓷厂）”的总经理，开始了筚路蓝缕的创业历程。当时的金鱼草刚刚起步，一切都需要从头开始，连生产什么产品都还没有确定。听闻这个消息后，谈志坚的四位老部下也毅然放弃了自己的工作，与老厂长一起从零开始创建金鱼草，盖厂房、进设备、招工人、搞培训、草拟工艺……每天几乎工作24个小时。1993年7月1日，宜兴金鱼陶瓷厂点火成功，并确立起“要把企业打造成陶瓷行业领军型企业”的宏伟蓝图。由此谈志坚重新回到陶瓷行业，开始了他新的人生旅程。

金鱼陶瓷厂开始时进口了马来西亚的设备，生产均陶大花盆，主要用于出口。在宜兴，均陶和紫砂一样拥有悠久的历史和良好的声誉，但在20世纪90年代，由于政治、经济等条件限制，加之均陶大花盆价格昂贵，金鱼陶瓷厂的发展并未达到谈志坚的预期目标，陷入了经营困境。不得已，谈志坚开始重新考察市场，调整自己的战略计划，最终决定，进军紫砂市场。那时宜兴紫砂已经拥有了相当高的知名度，容易被人们接受，但考虑到竞争者众多且不容易出新意，谈志坚并没有选择做紫砂壶及紫砂工艺品，而是剑走偏锋，有了一个大胆的创新想法：做紫砂酒瓶。

当时，全国各地出产优质陶土的地方很多，却只有宜兴出产紫砂陶土。紫砂陶土本色有红、黄、绿、棕、黑等，做成器皿后其表面会透露出若有若无的紫光。在中国的传统文化里，紫色代表着富贵与权势，紫砂器皿也因此独具一种高雅的气质。之所以称之为“砂”，是因为不管紫砂陶土磨得多细，其成品在细腻的外表下总给人以漂亮的立体“砂子”感，故得名。紫砂器皿质地坚细、色泽沉静、制作精美、清明古雅，传统的紫砂器皿外部一般不挂釉，烧造大多温度在1100℃～1180℃，成品大致可分为紫、褐、红、黑、黄、绿等色系。颜色烧成之后，不会褪色。

经过科学的分析，紫砂的原料中含有氧化铁、氧化铝、氧化镁、氧化钾、氧化钠、氧化铅、氧化锰等化学成分，多种矿物质组成的胎土属于高岭、石英、云母类型，适当的矿物质、化学组合、颗粒配合，使得紫砂的成品吸水率小于百分之二，气孔率介于一般的陶器、瓷器之间。这些紫砂

2

3

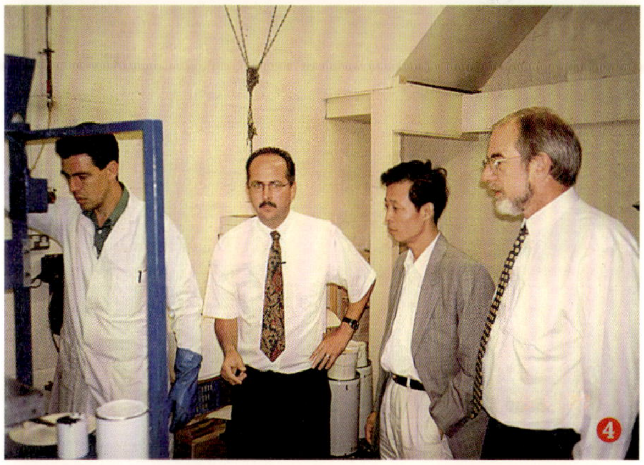
4

5

6

中华老字号

宜兴金鱼紫砂陶瓷酒瓶烧造技艺·老字号掌门人谈志坚

气孔分成闭口气孔和开口气孔两种，由于这种特殊的结构，使它具有了良好的透气性。茶水放于紫砂壶内，即使五六日不动也不会变馊。另外紫砂成品还有自然吐纳的特性，遇热气孔张开胎土将贮存之物吐出，贮油吐油、贮尘吐尘，贮茶吐茶香，所以用紫砂茶壶泡茶愈久愈香愈珍贵。

紫砂壶和即冲即饮的茶互相补益，相得益彰，为世人所喜爱。那么如果用紫砂做酒瓶储存窖藏美酒，会不会也有相同的效果呢？在谈志坚之前，曾有很多人也有过类似的想法，试图用紫砂来做酒瓶，但皆因无法解决紫砂器皿所特有的渗漏性，而被迫放弃。在他们看来，紫砂绝非制作酒瓶的良材，并告诫后人慎用此物。

谈志坚却不信这个邪，他通过科学的研究和分析，发现紫砂器皿渗水的根本原因在于传统的手工艺制作中不可避免的弊端和紫砂器皿烧制温度偏低等所致。所以要想解决紫砂器皿渗水的问题，就需要从这几方面入手。谈志坚的紫砂酒瓶研制方案就从材料筛选、研磨、选择先进的现代工艺设备等入手，采用了他在1991年用文片瓷（表面有裂纹）做酒瓶的技术，即在釉和胎之间加过渡层，从而解决了高温烧制紫砂器皿易开裂的技术难题。

紫砂器皿一经解决渗漏问题，做成酒瓶就只是时间问题了。由紫砂做成的酒瓶不仅拥有诸多玻璃及陶瓷酒瓶所共有的优点，还拥有许多它们所没有的长处。正如人们总结的那样，紫砂酒瓶有着六大特色：

一、经高温烧制，紫砂酒瓶物理化学稳定性高，即使长期存储，也不会发生酒水与周边环境发生化学反应的事情；

二、橡木桶贮藏葡萄酒催陈原因之一就是木桶具有透气又不渗漏的特性，紫砂酒瓶具有同样的特性，所以对酒精度相对较高的白酒原酒陈酿有着良好的催陈效果；

三、与玻璃瓶不同，紫砂酒瓶不透光，避免了光与酒的化学反应，可以很好地保持酒质；

四、相比玻璃等其他材质，紫砂酒瓶导热慢，可以长时间保持适中的酒温，既有酒窖藏酒的效果，又使酒越陈越香；

五、紫砂酒瓶取材于天然矿物，含有铁、铝、钠、钾、钙等元素，这些微量元素渗入酒中对人体有一定的保健作用；

六、紫砂本身具有的独特文化收藏特性和造型之美与酒的文化品位相得益彰，能带来可观的经济效益。

①

①⑤谈志坚工作照
②谈志坚陪同无锡市委常委、宜兴市委书记蒋洪亮（右一）视察金鱼陶瓷
③2011年谈志坚陪同宜兴政协代表团参观金鱼陶瓷
④谈志坚出席茅台集团白金酒礼行2010全国合作发展高峰论坛

经谈志坚设计改良后的紫砂酒瓶，工艺精湛，造型别致，色泽与图案古朴典雅，风格文静且有灵性，有种内敛含蓄、古朴温厚的魂魄。从经济效益来讲，紫砂酒瓶具有深厚的文化内涵和渊源，大大提升了酒的档次，深受酒厂特别是高档酒厂商的欢迎。它满足了高档酒厂商做高档收藏酒的需求，很快占领了国内市场。精美的紫砂酒瓶与醇香的美酒结合，更增加了彼此的艺术性与收藏性，推动了一股年份酒收藏投资的热潮。

谈志坚以自己独到的眼光和敏锐的判断，在陶瓷界为金鱼陶瓷赢得了良好的口碑和巨大的品牌效应，牢固树立了自己在陶瓷界的地位，赢得了一大批忠实的用户和合作者。2002年开始，谈志坚着力增加酒瓶的产量，全力占领高档白酒酒瓶市场。

在开发酒瓶市场的过程中，谈志坚对客户，始终坚持着五星级的服务。

五粮液酒厂在20世纪80年代初就有一个用陶瓷酒瓶装酒的梦想，21世纪初谈志坚帮五粮液圆了这个梦。谈志坚的理念是：中国的普通百姓喝一次五粮液不容易，配上高档品质的陶瓷酒瓶，一方面可以帮助消费者鉴别真假，一方面还可以帮助他们良好的收藏这些美酒。2005年谈志坚为五粮液开发了17万个高档陶瓷酒瓶，但灌装时五粮液酒厂觉得酒瓶质量有些不达标，谈志坚闻讯后，立即决定销毁全部成坯和酒瓶。酒瓶破裂的声音很清脆，谈志坚至今想来还犹在耳边，他说当时很多员工看着这些被砸碎的酒瓶心都碎了。但他却不以为然，着手开始重新组织生产，带领员工日夜奋战，到年底前为五粮液重新做了11万只超乎五粮液酒厂内控标准的优质酒瓶，圆了五粮液多年的梦。从此，五粮液酒厂与谈志坚建立起良好的合作关系。这次事件谈志坚单独承担了500万元的损失，但谈志坚的公司却从此开始实现从“鲫鱼”向“金鱼”的价值突变，在业界树立起了良好的信誉，成功打入了高端白酒的包装市场。

2005年谈志坚以超前的设计理念，超高的工艺要求，成功申请了色釉陶瓷酒瓶制备方法的专利，该发明专利确保了企业15年以上的技术优势，为自己的高档陶瓷酒瓶市场筑起了知识产权保护的长城。

毛泽东在新中国成立后对未能参加长征的陈毅说，四渡赤水是他军事指挥上的得意之笔。谈志坚喜欢对来访者讲，产品转型，大批量为著名品牌酒制作，供应高端陶瓷酒瓶，是他经营陶瓷企业的登峰之作。

21世纪，谈志坚总结其经商之道为“四赢”，即企业赢、客户赢、供货商赢、员工赢。企业盈利是生存的根本，谈志坚从技术、管理、销售等各个方面保证企业的正常盈利，并不断开拓创新；从1997年提出“双赢”开始，谈志坚就致力于培养优质客户，可以不惜代价供给潜力客户，客户发展起来后，谈志坚同样受益；对于供货商，谈志坚在要求供货商保证原材料质量的基础上，保证其利润空间，长期下来，谈志坚在供货商中赢得了良好的口碑，供货商以与谈志坚合作为信誉保障；谈志坚的员工工资水平一直居于同行最高水平，每月按时发放，并随着公司业绩的发展而适时上调，谈志坚的员工队伍稳定，鲜有跳槽发生。这一切成就了谈志坚今日在陶瓷界的地位与荣誉，也成就了他无与伦比的人格丰碑。

（三）宜兴金鱼紫砂陶瓷酒瓶烧造技艺守护者、掌门人谈珂

“青出于蓝而胜于蓝，承继传统而超越传统。”

谈珂，金鱼陶瓷现任掌门人，生长于陶瓷家庭之中，自小受父亲谈志坚的影响，对陶瓷生产特别是陶瓷酒瓶生产产生了浓厚的兴趣。

谈珂学习很好，一直没让父亲为自己操过心。只是在上大学报志愿计划填计算机专业时，父亲提出了反对意见，认为计算机更新快，经验不值钱，倒不如报考生物工程专业，那是真正朝阳产业，前景无限。谈珂没有采纳父亲的建议，按照自己本来的打算报考了计算机专业。

谈珂毕业后去了英国留学，专攻电子商务。学成归来，先后在无锡、上海的一些一流大企业工作，顺带炒炒股票，关注资本市场。

不管是去上大学还是去英国留学，谈珂都是自己在安排生活，自己在安排事业，这一方面是父亲独特的教育方式及对儿子充分信任的结果，另一方面谈珂也清楚自己该学什么，需要做什么。

学成归来，谈珂没有进入家族企业，而是去了无锡、上海，通过自己的努力先后进入了某些大型外企及国内知名的投资公司，做了自己需要了解的工作，学自己需要的东西。然而，不管是在国内还是国外，学习工作之余，谈珂最先关注的都是当地的陶瓷产品及陶瓷酒器，一有机会就去仔细了解它们的工艺特色、市场状况及该生产企业的发展脉络。所到之地及所能接触过的陶瓷产品及陶瓷酒器，他都能说出个一二三，并总结出各自的优劣。谈珂从没有刻意地做这些事情，他自己说是习惯使然。

与父亲的一次长谈，触发了谈珂心底的激情，谈珂决定回到陶瓷酒器行业，继续父亲的事业与梦想，当然这也是谈珂自己的梦想，他要让陶瓷酒器朝着现代化方向发展，并要深入挖掘陶瓷酒器的文化内涵。这种激情是一种理智的回归，是对陶瓷事业源自心底的热爱，是在经历了中外文化碰撞、现代化企业进程洗礼后具有责任感与使命感的理性回归。

与父亲略有不同，谈珂虽不像父亲那样懂得陶瓷酒器的每个环节，但他更懂得如何让不同的人发挥不同的作用，熟谙如何驾驭团队合作，他的创新思路也更加的开阔。谈珂要让陶瓷酒器走得更远，不再向父辈那样默默耕耘，他要汇聚各界的力量提升陶瓷酒器的文化品位；他要与各大院校进行更广范围更深层次的合作，进

①掌门人谈珂近影

掌门人档案

谈珂

中华老字号宜兴金鱼紫砂陶瓷酒瓶烧造技艺守护者、掌门人

宜兴市金鱼陶瓷有限公司副总经理

中华老字号

宜兴金鱼紫砂陶瓷酒瓶烧造技艺·掌门人谈珂

行更广泛的创新；他计划开展展览活动，与北大等院校合作，邀请考古界、收藏界人士交流经验；他要举办设计大赛，网络人才，集思广益，征询创新设计，提高紫砂陶瓷酒器的知名度……

年轻的谈珂比谈志坚更加激进，他不满足于一年几千万的利润，他认为既然已经在业界做成了第一品牌，利润、规模、客户群都已比较稳定而且具有相当的规模，那么完全有实力进行再投资或是上市，有必要加速前进，让他们的产品、企业永立潮头，特别要让他们的紫砂陶瓷酒器成为真正举世皆知的艺术品，才能不被后来者赶超。

每个成功的企业及传人都有近乎相同的经历，李嘉诚凭着多年勤奋及个人才华的积累，创造出一段惊世财富传奇；李泽钜学成归来加入父亲公司，勤勉低调，在10年间将家族资产放大数倍，继续书写财富梦想。

在上学期间，谈珂就曾经到父亲的企业打工，戏称“票了一把”。那时谈珂从自己所学专业入手，结合父亲公司的情况，致力于为企业初步建立一套信息化的管理系统。与父亲沟通后，谈珂的想法很快实施起来。谈珂邀请几位同学为企业初步建立了一套电子化数据管理系统，使库存数据及生产报表等信息实现电子化操作，大大节省了人力物力，也使得数据更加的真实准确，此后这套系统沿用了三年，目前部分功能仍在继续发挥作用。

2006年春，谈珂正式进入父亲的企业，这次他没有从自己擅长的电子商务入手，也没有进入管理层，此时的谈珂更加的理智与成熟，他跟父亲约定，先从基层慢慢做起，从普通员工做起，熟悉每一道工序，系统了解陶瓷的生产工艺与制作流程。在将近两年的时间里谈珂一个个车间走过来，从原料、模型、成型、窑务到手彩、贴花、检验车间，一道道工序从产品报表、岗位工人数量、岗位职责都作了详尽的记录分析，他观察每一位员工，为企业选拔储备人才。谈珂说：“必须有这样一个过程，毕竟做陶瓷行业，不然什么都不懂讲话都像门外汉一样的。”

经过两年的基层锻炼，谈珂对企业有了自己的认识与发展规划。

谈珂进入父亲的公司已有6年时间，俨然是“老员工”了。相比大学期间的“打工票友”，如今谈珂对公司情况已经了然于胸：跟他谈陶瓷，他会把每道工序的专业技法流程、烧造要点、员工配备深入浅出娓娓道出；跟他谈企业管理，他会从供应链、财务会计、生产制造、成本、人力资源讲到办公用品，从标准建立讲到

1

①②谈珂近影
③谈珂参加金鱼陶瓷与清华大学美术学院合作签约仪式
④2011年9月谈珂参加茅台名将酒品鉴会
⑤2011年4月谈珂参加汾酒供货商大会

业绩考核，合情合理；他更加注重品牌建设、青瓷文化挖掘，他更倾向汇集社会的力量，让企业走得更远……

家族公司由于历史及固有的客观原因在管理及发展方式上多存在某些不足。谈珂也不断研究总结公司的现状，他认为在管理方面公司现有的领导团体不适合未来发展的趋势，比如父亲谈志坚精通陶瓷、企业管理及财务，堪称全才，他没必要配备副总，也不需要智囊团，但企业发展至今，并要不断扩大的时候，急需一个强有力的领导团队，各司其职，团结协作。在父亲的支持下，谈珂紧锣密鼓地组建新的管理团队，从公司各个岗位输送、从大中专院校录取培养，充实到公司科研、市场、财务等各个领域，目前正在进行第三梯队的选拔培养。

限于各种原因公司的发展方式比较粗放，谈珂规划把企业的发展方向导航到集约化、信息化道路上来，派人专门负责收集研讨相关资料，逐步把生产中的设计、烧造等工艺流程、人力资源管理、销售体系流程化正规化；继续开发生产、销售电子信息管理系统，建立公司内网，实现信息化管理，提升企业现代化水平，提高效率，节约人力物力财力。

在现代的经济环境下，一个好的企业管理者不一定是全才，事事精通，重要的是他要懂得用人之道，深知什么人在什么领域能做得最好，还应懂得怎样是做好了，怎样是不及格。无疑，谈珂已经拥有了这样的储备。谈珂深知自己不像父亲做陶瓷出身，不能像父亲那样细致地了解青瓷，但他懂得如何把企业做得更大更强，知道谁可以帮自己做陶瓷，更知道谁可以帮自己实现青瓷和传承金鱼紫砂陶瓷酒瓶的梦想。

如果说谈志坚完成了企业的第一次创业，为将来打下了坚实的基础，那么谈珂此时就是以第二次创业者的身份出现，他面临的是企业可持续发展的问题，需要以科学的态度与方法，实现企业的第二次创业，要抛弃原有的经验做法，推陈出新，以新的管理模式代替旧的管理模式，尽快解决诸如组织机制障碍、人力资源限制、决策程序不规范等种种问题，重新建立起一个依靠企业整体素质来实现持续发展的管理体系，这场变革对企业对个人来说都是一个脱胎换骨的过程。

在谈珂的建议下，企业在北京的文化宣传公司正式成立，主要负责企业的对外展览与销售联络，该公司由谈珂全权负责。在培养新的企业领导集团方面，第二、第三、第四梯队建设培养也由谈珂全程操控。借鉴国外及其他行业的成功经验，谈珂计划把公司厂区建设成集生产、旅游观光、文化展览于一体的碧玉青瓷和金鱼紫砂陶瓷酒瓶工业园区。

为实现父亲与自己的青瓷梦想，谈珂邀请学术、实践、院校、一线工人、文化公司等各界人士深入挖掘陶瓷酒器的文化内涵，把陶瓷酒器真正做大做强。

谈珂曾经表露，在实现计划时，遇到的最大问题是执行力的问题。一是管理层不健全，执行起来有阻力，新来的有能力的“空降”管理层与公司及员工需要一定的磨合过程，一是新的发展思路与固有的发展模式的摩擦，存在观念的碰撞。这样的问题是每一个改革者必须要面临的问题，此时不仅需要耐力，更需要坚持，需要领导者具有足够的抗压能力，需要与时俱进，做各方冲击下的中流砥柱，稳稳把住企业的航向，乘风破浪！

三、重要传承人口述实录

（一）谈志坚口述实录

采访人：王晶（略为“王”）

被采访人：谈志坚（略为“谈”）

采访时间：2009年10月29日

采访地点：宜兴市金鱼陶瓷有限公司

王：谈总您好，您是哪年生人？目前在金鱼陶瓷厂担任什么职位？

谈：我出生于1954年9月。目前担任宜兴市金鱼陶瓷有限公司董事长。

王：您在哪里读书？请简述一下家族的情况。

谈：我初中毕业于宜兴市杨巷中学，大学毕业于南京工业大学（前身为：南京化工学院）陶瓷专业。家族情况：父母为工人阶级出身，初解放时为干部家庭。姐、妹均为工人；夫人与我是大学同学，也毕业于陶瓷专业，目前在环保局负责环境监测工作；儿子谈珂毕业于英国布鲁奈尔大学（硕士学位），从2006年起，任宜兴市金鱼陶瓷有限公司副总经理并负责管理多家公司，曾被评为第七届“中国经济百名杰出人物”、“宜兴市青年创业明星”、“陶都宜兴优秀青年陶艺家”。

王：您是哪年开始学习制作陶瓷酒瓶？在宜兴还有别的企业也在做陶瓷酒瓶吗？

谈：我于1970年分配到宜兴瓷厂（宜兴青瓷厂的前身），当时企业也零散做一些青瓷酒瓶，但批量不大。1978年，我毕业于南京化工学院（陶瓷专业），学成归来后便加入宜兴青瓷厂，开始从事具体的陶瓷技术工作，自1984年担任宜兴青瓷厂副厂长后，开始真正研究陶瓷酒瓶制作技艺。1985年首先设计并改进了陶瓷酒瓶的上釉装置，之后逐步对传统的制作技艺与装备进行了一系列的技术改良，大大降低了生产成本，提高了劳动效率，实现了产量与利润的突破式增长：自1985年开始批量生产陶瓷酒瓶，1992年的产量达到了800多万只。

80年代中期，仅宜兴青瓷厂一家在做陶瓷酒瓶，另有一些企业做的是酒坛、酒瓮等酒器，以及普通的黄酒陶瓷酒瓶。目前，宜兴地区已有四、五十家企业在制作陶瓷酒瓶，其中，金鱼陶瓷酒瓶的产量占40%左右，产值占50%以上。

王：咱们金鱼陶瓷酒瓶的生产起源，是自创还是外来传播？

谈：金鱼陶瓷酒瓶属于自创生产。1993年，“金鱼陶瓷”吸收并延续了原宜兴青瓷厂制作青瓷酒瓶的成功经验并在此基础上，对原料、釉料、模具、设备、窑炉装置、烧成温度、工艺流程等原有制作工艺进行了全方位的技术改良，继而形成了“金鱼陶瓷酒瓶”独树一帜的、自成一体的制作工艺与生产模式。

王：在当地，还有哪些老字号制作酒瓶的流派吗？

谈：目前，在本地没有其他老字号制作酒瓶的流派。

王：金鱼陶瓷酒瓶制作技艺的目前现状如何？

谈：通过长期的经验积累与技术改进，目前金鱼陶瓷酒瓶的制作技艺已经达到国内外最先进的工艺水平，成为我国陶瓷酒瓶行业标准的第一起草单位，引领了整个陶瓷酒瓶制作行业和高端白酒包装行业的发展。

王：宜兴的自然资源为金鱼陶瓷酒瓶的制作提供了哪些物质条件和便利？

谈：宜兴地区丰富的陶土资源固然为金鱼陶瓷酒瓶的制作提供了最基础的原料来源，然而最根本、最重要的是：宜兴地区历经千百年发展的源远流长的陶瓷文化，以及多品种陶瓷制作技艺的相互融合渗透，形成了当地独有的文化传统、经济形态、制作技巧以及劳动力资源，共同为金鱼陶瓷酒瓶的制作创造了得天独厚的“天时、地利、人和”等多方面的有利条件。

王：宜兴的运输情况如何？酒瓶都是通过什么渠道运送？

谈：宜兴位于江浙沪交界地带，交通十分便利，目前的酒瓶都是通过汽车货运的渠道进行运输。

王：金鱼陶瓷酒瓶传统技艺生产方式现在与之前有哪些变化？

谈：金鱼陶瓷酒瓶在继承传统制作技艺的同时，坚持不懈地对传统技艺与生产方式进行了改革创新以适应时代和市场发展的需求：例如，我们是第一家将过去传统的倒焰窑和隧道窑改造为辊道窑的企业，窑炉改革的成功大大提高了生产力与销售量；我们将一体成型的对开模具改良为分隔成型的模具，改进了开模方法；将低温素烧、高温釉烧改为一次高温釉烧，又将陶瓷酒瓶里、外釉一次烧成改为分别烧成，使酒瓶的釉质表面呈现出如同玻璃般的镜面效果，达到了外部装饰基本无缺陷的工艺要求；在酒瓶瓶头的生产工艺中由注浆法、滚压加工法发展到利用粉末干压、切削加工技术等，大大提高了陶瓷酒瓶口与塞的密封效果。目前，金鱼陶瓷酒瓶的生产规模与工艺技术已实现了产业化和标准化，始终处于国内领先水平。

王：金鱼陶瓷酒瓶传统制作技艺与现代科技之间，关系是什么？

谈：事实上，金鱼陶瓷酒瓶的传统制作技艺与现代科技是密不可分的。陶瓷酒瓶的传统制作技艺是前人通过长期实践积累的宝贵经验，是祖辈们智慧和创意的结晶，直到现在仍是值得我们学习和继承的。同时，我们还通过科学的管理理念、先进的工艺流程和现代化的技术装备，对传统的制作技艺进行改革和创新，以利于进一步提高劳动效率、提高产品质量并提高环保水平，如此才能做到兼容并蓄、不断发展。

王：金鱼陶瓷酒瓶目前有多少种类？服务单位有哪些？

谈：目前，金鱼陶瓷酒瓶的品种造型达2000～3000多个，近年来，每年设计开发新样400～600余款，常年生产品种多达300多个，其中每年投入生产的有近100个。服务的单位主要有：贵州茅台酒股份有限公司、宜宾五粮液酒业有限责任公司、中国泸州老窖股份有限公司、陕西西凤酒股份有限公司、安徽口子酒业股份有限公司、酒鬼酒股份有限公司、四川郎酒集团有限责任公司、山西杏花村汾酒厂股份有限公司、古越龙山、辽宁道光廿五集团满族酿酒有限责任公司、安徽文王酿酒股份有限公司、安徽双轮酒业股份有限公司、安徽迎驾贡酒有限公司、伊犁肖尔布拉克酒业有限责任公司、吉林省榆树钱酒业有限公司、云南金六福酒业有限公司、陕西泸康酒业（集团）股份有限公司、广西丹泉酒业有限公司、安徽井中集团店小二酿酒有限公司、四川绵竹剑南春酒厂有限公司、河南宋河酒业股份有限公司、内蒙古奥淳酒业有限责任公司、内蒙古河套酒业集团股份有限公司、湖南武陵酒有限公司、四川省绵阳市丰谷酒业有限责任公司、甘肃金徽酒业有限责任公司、浙江老台门酒业销售有限公司等。

王：金鱼陶瓷酒瓶的各种制作方法，造型，您是否都掌握？

谈：是的，很多造型与成型方法都是由我亲自设计与创新的，并掌握着各种制作方法及工艺。

王：宜兴地方是否对金鱼酒瓶传统制作技艺的传承创造了物质条件？

谈：是的，宜兴当地政府十分支持金鱼陶瓷酒瓶对传统技艺的传承与发展，并提供了多项有利的政策支持，将陶瓷酒瓶的制作列为高新技术项目以及文化产业资金引导项目，并给予了配套的资金支持，为金鱼陶瓷酒瓶的发展提供了物质条件和保障。

王：您招聘工人有什么讲究或者相关的条件？

谈：肯做、肯学，最重要的是热爱陶瓷行业，愿意投身于这个行业。陶瓷行业博大精深，本身涉及到多方面的学科知识并且是互通的，所以我认为做这一行并不存在专业方面的技术壁垒，所有人只要肯努力、肯付出，就可以成为陶瓷行业的人才。

王：金鱼陶瓷酒瓶销售的范围以及情况。

谈：多年来，“金鱼陶瓷”与茅台、五粮液、泸州老窖、西凤酒、郎酒、酒鬼酒、汾酒、安徽口子窖等国内众多一流名酒企业常年保持良好合作，当前金鱼陶瓷酒瓶的销售分布已基本覆盖全国，包括：北京、天津、河北、湖北、湖南、四川、广东、黑龙江、山东、陕西、新疆、浙江、安徽、辽宁、台湾、江西、山西、贵州、江苏、上海、云南、西藏、内蒙古、青海等各省市地区。

王：金鱼陶瓷酒瓶传统制作技艺在全球化，现代化，城市化过程中面临哪些危机？技艺传承的主要困难是什么？

谈：目前，陶瓷酒瓶的生产制作可说是朝阳产业，它带动了高端白酒的包装革命，提升了白酒行业的形象品位与经济效益，发展前景仍十分广阔。然而从一定意义上讲，陶瓷酒瓶并非最终消费品，它需要依托白酒行业的发展，因此，陶瓷酒瓶的经济效益往往受其制约。从事陶瓷酒瓶制作这一传统行业的工作环境及条件通常比较艰苦，目前，技艺传承的主要困难是人才的缺乏，尤其是高学历、高素质人才的匮乏。

王：金鱼陶瓷酒瓶在本地，本行业口碑如何？乡亲或者同行是如何评价的？

谈：金鱼陶瓷酒瓶在本地同行及乡亲中始终拥有良好的口碑，工艺技术、发展规模都处于行业内的领先水平，并且带动了本地陶瓷酒瓶产业集群的发展，被业内同仁誉为日用陶瓷生产企业中的“航空母舰”。

王：您在宜兴本地的影响主要有哪些方面？

谈：首先是带动了本地陶瓷酒瓶行业的发展：通过在陶瓷酒瓶生产制作方面推行的一系列改革创新，形成了除紫砂产业之外的陶都宜兴最大的陶瓷产业群体；其次，在一定程度上推动了区域经济的发展：1993年，宜兴地区只有“金鱼陶瓷”一家生产紫砂陶瓷酒瓶，到目前为止已发展到近50家生产企业，销售规模已达10亿元，并带动了全国其他产区进军酒瓶行业的发展趋势。2011年，企业销售收入突破4亿元，上交国、地两税3200余万元；此外，对社会的发展作出了一份贡献：目前，“金鱼陶瓷”已安置了2600多名工人上岗生产，其中包括200多名残疾人员，员工的工资收入始终处于本地同行中的最高水平；自2007年起，分20年捐赠慈善机构300万元，已连续四年兑现支付，并向当地居民和敬老院奉献爱心。

王：您是否靠金鱼陶瓷酒瓶的制作作为主要的经济收入？

谈：是的，甚至可以说金鱼陶瓷酒瓶的制作是我全部的经济收入。因为我没有投资其他项目，也不去炒股或炒基金。

（二）谈珂口述实录

采访人：孙冬宁（略为“孙”）

被采访人：谈珂（略为“谈”）

文字记录：何梁

采访时间：2010年8月23日

采访地点：宜兴市金鱼陶瓷有限公司

孙：谈总哪年生人？

谈：1980年10月份。

孙：你从小开始上学都是在宜兴？

谈：对，我是1980年生人，从上小学开始一直在宜兴读书。

孙：宜兴？不是在丁山？

谈：是宜兴。我从小跟姥姥住在一起，基本上见不上我父亲的面，他一直在丁山创业的。

孙：这也跟南方的文化教育有关，父母都希望孩子住在条件好点的地方。基本上都是这样子的，你对你的孩子，是不是也会采取这样一种方式呢？

谈：有可能，我的孩子，我也不想让他待在太小的城市，还要出去到大城市，包括到国外学习。

孙：你大学在哪里读的？什么专业？

谈：南京大学计算机专业。具体叫计算机科学技术。计算机科学与技术是一个系。具体是软件，我当时学的是软件。

孙：你是哪年入学的？

谈：1999年到2003年。

孙：2003年以后呢？

谈：2003年之后我就到英国去学习了一年。读的电子商务，硕士研究生。到2004年底12月份回来了，当中有一年半的时间在英国。

孙：你觉得这一年半的海外留学背景对你目前的各种状态，有什么影响？

谈：有很多观念上的转变。包括一些生活的态度、思维方式，这些跟国内还是有些地方不一样。

孙：思维方式不一样，就会对你的观念产生很大冲突。

谈：是的。中国人比较重视一板一眼啊，比较在乎我过得怎么样我要成功，就是给别人看的。但老外他没有这种感觉，他只要自己活得开心舒服就行。生活充满幸福感，他们强调自我发展。在国内生活，每天一下来，压力很大，生活很累。因为中国从小的教育就是一种成功式的教育。但老外他们就是一种，比如说，有人的理想是我要做一个卡车司机。在中国人的教育当中，肯定说，小孩子怎么能有这样一种理想？老外他不是这样，老外从小教育小孩的是，自我的一种价值的体现，怎么在人生中克服一些困难。他不去教育一个孩子长大后成为什么样的人，他不是这种意识教育。所以这方面，中西文化可能存在很大差异。

孙：那么宜兴或者丁山区域，这种意识的最大区别是什么？

谈：宜兴人的思想观念，包括一些开放程度跟大城市都有很大区别。感觉很费力。从上到下有一点想守的味道，就是比较保守，有一点小富即安的味道，一年赚个几千万利润也差不多了，也不想再把盘子做大，也不想上市等等问题。所以我一直在逼着他们往前走，说企业后面有追兵，既然做成第一品牌了，那今后的发展更重要。后面的人把我们当目标，肯定是很快就追上。我们是在第一个目标，只能跑得更快！我们有时候也要故意培养一个敌人、或者说是目标，这样才能更好地促进我们的发展。

孙：什么原因促使你参与家族企业的创建？

谈：有一次我和父亲聊天的时候，他说这么大的摊子做到后来怎么样呢，再做个多少年，父亲做不动了，我也不做，还有那么多人要吃饭呢。这样一甩手不管了，破产了。我们的生活没有问题，厂里还有这么多兄弟姐妹们，也要对他们负责啊。我感受到了父亲身上背负的责任。我告诉父亲既然这样，我回来接班从头学起，英国也好上海也罢，人总是要有个理想。此时，父亲的责任已经渗透到我的理想当中。

孙：这中间将有一个漫长的衔接过程。

谈：对，考虑到如果要接班，晚回来还不如早一点回来，深入基层工作，学习企业管理也要几年的工夫。几年下来正好也三十几岁，慢慢把这个团队先交接起来。

孙：从某种程度上讲，你跟你父亲也是一个合作伙伴。

谈：我积极地向我父亲学习。我父亲是上一代的领导核心，他们那一代是紧紧围绕我父亲，因为我父亲什么都懂，手下的人只需要按照他的指示做事情就已经很好了。我跟老谈总的这种管理模式不一样了，我本身不是这个专业出身，需要一个配合团队一起协商，决策今后的一些战略计划。

孙：你刚到公司的时候有职务吗？

谈：没有职务。刚到公司的时候就在车间里面待了一年多。一个个车间跑过来的。原料、模型、成型，然后到窑务，以前还有手彩车间，然后后面就是所有的工序了解一下，你必须有这样一个过程，不然你什么都不懂你讲话都是门外汉一样的。

孙：一个车间平均要两到三个月，哪个车间你待的时间最长？

谈：成型车间，就是这个坯子的成型。前面原料时间短一点，因为它就是一个配方。

孙：这些过程是一个非常好的经历。熟悉完车间以后又是什么工作？

谈：车间完了以后就开始筹建我们另外一个酒瓶新车间，筹建新的车间之后在那边负责了一段时间，相当于一个副车间主任。在这个位置做了半年多一点时间。就开始做生产副总，就是管生产。管了也是一两年吧，具体时间好像要到去年。

孙：你还记得第一天来金帆上班的时间吗？

谈：记得。我以前的寒暑假都回来公司帮帮忙，实践一下。

孙：你第一次实践是什么时候？

谈：大二。我在大学里面找了两个大四的同学，给我们这边做生产报表。一种电子化的东西，解决了原来的人工录入的问题。

孙：你潜意识里有种意识关注着公司的情况。

谈：当时我在系里面认识几个师兄，就请教他们能不能做一些库存、生产报表等等电子化的软件。后来陆陆续续做了一些，用了两三年。

孙：软件应该逐渐升级，他们做的软件升级跟得上吗？

谈：没有升级，所以随着企业发展，那时候的软件都淘汰了。现在我正跟金蝶软件沟通，他们也来公司进行了一些摸底工作，我们准备把生产、销售，包括采供、库存这四个模块，逐渐实现电子化。

孙：从这个角度你的意识比老谈总要强烈。这两天我们在拍酒瓶子的照片，很多原来的资料都找不到了。从你来了以后。才有意识的保留一点电子版的图纸，效果图、图片之类。

谈：对，我回来以后，让我英国的朋友过来帮我来筹建信息部门，我要建立一个信息收集中心。我把一些大事记重新整理一遍，原来都没人系统梳理。就比如原来企业的一些历程是什么，都没有。这些都应该是记录的很扎实的一种企业文化。包括内网，我都想搞起来，我们企业的一些资料啊，包括今年发生的一些什么重要的事情啊，都要往里面录。所以，这次的东西工作做完之后，那又可以成为企业的一个大事记，又可以录进去了。包括我们投的一个新厂，今年那1月份到6月份竣工，都弄进去。

孙：把有效资料很好地保存下来，是家族企业一脉相承的最好见证。

谈：对，虽然现在厂里有档案室，但是更多的是注重于企业荣誉方面材料管理和一些人力档案。我们还需要很多方面的材料保管，逐步完成市场信息部。

孙：企业每年接受大量的设计图纸，文化类的设计订单，包括设计师带的很多样品，这些东西的话，你们现在是怎么整理？

谈：现在在金鱼陶瓷，有一个小潘专门负责整理这些东西。配备了电脑、服务器。以前也注意这些，以前设计公司过来也是一张图纸，他也没有电脑，是近两年这些要求上去了之后，随着科技发展了，流程才开始正规化。我们也经历了一个从粗放型到正规化的管理过程。所以我决定用半年时间，通过金蝶来个调研，把整个生产体系，包括库存、采供、销售这一摊子，从销售到计划，下订单开始，包括他出样开始，就是全实行电子化统一管理，这样可以省掉很多人力成本。

孙：这一方面你预计规划和实施大约要多长时间？

谈：如果全部弄好起码要半年，就是四个模块。当然我们以后还可以实现一个人力资源的模块，考核的模块。ERP系统它可以是一个一个模块做，因为你这样子的话，也是慢慢的投入。你要一下子一个项目整个铺开的话，一百多万，有的两三百万挡不住，投入太大。

孙：陶瓷生产的电子化实现起来简单吗？

谈：我们先把最繁琐的工作，比方说生产系统先实现，然后再销售系统再实现，库存反正是很简单。再把采购、人力资源，包括考核这些都可以慢慢实现。现在你比方算工资都是按月算，那么你一天做了一千两百，一个月做多少？每个月到20号之前他要算账。以后的话我只要把数字一敲进去，因为定额的话我只要设置一下，比方说这个瓶子五毛钱，自动一乘，看出来了。现在都要一笔笔的人工算，很繁琐，浪费了金鱼的人力财力。现在我们平均一个车间要配到两个专门的计算员，那叫统计人员。今后的话，说实话，我全电脑的，我都不需要人了。只要一个统计员，就是数字每天电脑上录入一下，就一个录入人员，也不要算账，就很方便。我们看到的报表，他将是一个汇总表，没有电子化前是通过一道一道车间上来，我们看到的报表是三天前的了，都不是实时的。

孙：咱们的紫砂陶瓷酒瓶属于领跑地位。你对目前这一行业的发展，有什么发展的规划和议程？

谈：我认为中端的市场有很大的量，各个行业是一个金字塔形，下面量最大，但是价格实在太低。高端的价格很好，量毕竟有限。但中端这一部分就是十块左右到十五块左右这些瓶子，既有量，又有利润空间，所以这部分是我们今后一个发展的趋势，我们逐步把低端的瓶放出去给一些其他的小厂做。包括以后或者可能上市之后，采取一些收购行动。收购了以后技术扶持，把它培养起来，专门做低端的一些瓶，我们总部要扩张制作中端酒瓶。现在从我们公司结构来说，高端瓶一年五六百万个，但是中端瓶也就四五百万个，比高端瓶还少，原因是我们接不下那么多单子。我们低端瓶子一年要做两三千万。

孙：目前国内高端酒瓶市场当中，我们能排到第几位？

谈：排前三没有问题。还有两家，其中有一家湖南做白瓷的现在做高端酒瓶，之前是做出口餐具，都是做酒器跟瓷器的，他们的坯体一直是一种白瓷的，就是很单一。还有重庆的华陶，华陶原来是国营的，现在它的董事长叫张明，现在华陶景晖也改成自己的企业了。原来华陶国营厂的时候是做出口居多，他主要做瓷器的骨瓷。当时也是四川省的重点企业，投资设备全是国外进口的。

孙：现在的高端酒瓶市场，我们市场持有量能达到百分之多少？这几家的技术水平怎么评定？

谈：技术实力来说，湖南那家瓷器做得比较好。酒瓶品种比较少，他主要做一个舍得跟红花郎。持有量多少具体数字没统计过。我们所说的高端酒瓶是二十几块钱的，现在真正就业内来说，能达到这个价格的也就我们。华陶的红花郎十六块，舍得十二块多，这个价位对于我们来说就是中端。

孙：我们在进行资本运营之后，是不是有希望兼顾一部分中端酒瓶市场，推动品牌发展？

谈：对。中端的量是很大的。中端的量比目前说的高端酒瓶量要多好几倍。

孙：还要做出我们的特色。

谈：现在有很多酒厂，例如汾酒做的定制酒瓶，一千多块钱一个，十八斤装。他是拿去拍卖的。只要九十八个瓶子。这种单子虽然价格好，但是一般的厂商根本没法做。九十八个瓶子你怎么做？但是我们赔本也要做好。打品牌就是要做别的厂做不了的酒瓶。我们现在越来越多的这种类型的大瓶子他拿去拍卖也好、展厅里放着也好、送礼也好，这一部分现在有一些上升的趋势。这种属于特别高端。

孙：这些特别高端的酒瓶实际上就等于酒瓶艺术品。

谈：相当于酒瓶中的艺术奢侈品。他装的酒就是酒中奢侈品。

孙：金鱼这个品牌现在已经成为陶瓷酒瓶的知名品牌了。

谈：金鱼在酒厂那边和设计公司那边，是全国公认的品牌。酒厂找设计公司做效果图，他也要咨询设计公司我去哪可以做到？设计公司一般来说，你达到这个效果，不计成本，不考虑价格的话，首选金鱼。

孙：从资本运营的这个角度，你考虑过上市问题，在这部分你有什么样的规划和想法？

谈：我们计划是想一年到两年的时间，以现有的两个公司为主体，快速实现上市问题。但是在接洽过程中发现了一些历史沿革的问题不是能够快速处理好的，还要涉及一些这几年的账目和税收问题。要做到正规运作。这一部分的补充工作要耽误一些时间，我跟父亲商量定一个远期的目标。就三年到四年时间，成立一个新的股份有限公司，把所有的业务销售全部做到里面。或者如何把这两个企业打包重组，金帆就做餐具，金鱼做酒瓶，还有一个青瓷。如果按照现在这个规划三到四年的时间够用了，之后可以进驻一些有实力的投资行业。

我回来几年跟我爸提出来一个建议，既然企业那么好，利润也达到了，规模也达到了，全国的一流的酒厂都是我们的客户群。在这些条件都很好的条件下，已经具备了一些上市、融资等等再发展的条件。如果再投资别的产业，已经具备一些技术能力。比方说我们目前要完成的金帆大厦，为什么还要自己拿出钱来去建造呢？完全可以上市之后，融资再实现我们的愿望。有目的地去做，反而还可以让企业更好地运转。在这方面，我父亲跟我观点不一样。

孙：你谈的一个例子很好。涉及一个诺基亚跟西门子之间的一个差距，把目前金帆在陶瓷界的位置喻为西门子。你在西门子工作多长时间？

谈：不到一年时间。我03年7月份毕业去了英国，04年底回国。05年整个一年都在西门子公司。

孙：当时没想到英国发展？

谈：英国它本身是一个非移民国家。这个国家是一个老欧洲的国家，现在已经进入一种停滞不前的状态，相对来说，一些发展的机会反而没有国内多，就业也很困难。在英国是节奏很慢的一个国家，感觉它在逐渐没落。

孙：从英国回来以后先到上海？

谈：先到无锡，西门子公司。到西门子公司一两年的时间，我都在无锡，上海只是去了三四个月。

孙：在西门子公司你具体从事哪方面的工作？

谈：我做了一段的销售。无锡市西门子真空管有限公司，做高压电线上高压开关的真空管。

孙：你在这一块西门子销售做了多长时间？

谈：做了，差不多一年。

孙：去上海工作是无锡西门子公司的业务关系吗？还是跳槽到其他单位？

谈：跳槽。西门子是国际化的大公司。分工很细，真正进去学到的东西比较少。你像我们公司销售科，有一个员工专门就做合同的。分工很明确，如果你负责跟客户沟通联系，下订单，你就只接触客户，其他的事情你都接触不了。那做合同的就是做合同的，他就是一直在那做。我跳槽到小公司是想多学点东西，公司小这个事情没人做，你要做，那个事情没人做你也做，这样对个人的成长，反而是一种锻炼。

孙：你最近忙什么？

谈：工作之余我正在进行专业化游泳训练。

孙：你觉得在工作之余，运动最重要？

谈：运动很重要。我平时没什么其他的爱好，有时候会打打羽毛球，打打台球。运动可以让人充分释放体力，是另一种放松。

孙：是的。运动是体力的修正。我看你们团队整体上很年轻，老谈总也是有意识地给你配了一批相对年轻的管理阶层。

谈：对，现在已经意识到我们的管理层，中间有一个断层，年龄从50多岁一下子跨越到二三十岁。这个中间其实是有一个断层，因为当时公司是集体的企业，老谈总一个人管理。他没注重培养副职，也没有培养中高层。但改制之后他突然发现，近几年管理人才是一种青黄不接的感觉。所以这两年我们是陆陆续续从各个陶瓷厂，包括一些管理学校、高校，找一些管理型、技术型、开发型的这种人才。

孙：你们现在这个年轻的管理团队有多少人？你觉得正常运营过程中，管理人员应该有多少人？

谈：我们从最早的06、07年开始意识到这个问题，开始招这方面的人。然后每年招十个左右，陆陆续续地遴选淘汰，大浪淘沙之后，现在真正能留下来几个，基本上能够独当一面。

孙：现在除了酒瓶之外金鱼还有生产其他的跟酒有关的器具吗？

谈：我除了做酒具，还做一些食品罐装坛子等等，包括一些酒器和食品的包装容器。酒器的话范围就大多了。

孙：那你觉得我们现在这个"瓶"字要不要改成"器"字？金鱼紫砂陶瓷酒器，这牵扯跟以后文化品牌汇合问题。建设文化品牌这部分，你们下一步有什么样的规划？

谈：我们目前跟高等院校结合起来做项目就是要延伸我们的文化品牌。去年跟清华大学签了五年合作协议，清华大学负责设计，我们来烧制。今后还打算做一系列的品茶的杯子或者公道杯之类。不定期地做展览，或者策划一些设计比赛，从中得到好的作品。一个品牌的文化打造不是一朝一夕的事情。

孙：在这个过程之中要考虑多方面问题，你马上作为新时期的掌门人，你觉得跟老一代掌门人之间最大区别是什么？

谈：最主要还是观念不一样。因为年龄和阅历的不同，他们更多的是守，我更多的是进攻。

孙：工作五年以来，你觉得最大的困难是什么？

谈：最大的工作困难是下面的执行力问题。

孙：我们可以把紫砂陶瓷酒瓶的制造流程作为特色文化旅游产品。

谈：我们也去英国、德国、美国等地考察，看过他们的陶瓷产业，他们就是集生产、展出、工业旅游于一体，很多日本人，亚洲人都跑到英国的当时的薇吉伍德，他有个工业园区嘛，就是工业旅游一条线的，就是可以去参观他们的制作流程，他们后面是生产，工厂是密封的，但是前面有一个具体的生产过程展示。

孙：就是前店后厂的形式。

谈：对，他是这种形式的。我们也尝试开发工业旅游这部分。

孙：谢谢！

啓後人

民间文学与诗赋

1 男欢女嬉

中华老字号

宜兴金鱼紫砂陶瓷酒瓶烧造技艺·民间文学与诗赋

一、与宜兴陶瓷酒器相关的民间故事、民间传说

茅台酒坛的故事

酒坛是我们经常看到的酒器之一，它以肚子大、呼吸性好、能储酒，深受广大爱酒者的喜爱。

可是它也有不好的地方，甚至险些让我们的国酒茅台沦为无人知晓的二三流品牌。事情是这样的，当年在万国博览会上，茅台酒被摆在一个不起眼的角落里，这里很少有人问津。古朴的酒坛子和毫无华彩可言的外表，几乎无法吸引那些喜欢华丽外表的参观者眼球。眼看着别人的展台人满为患，自己的展台却门可罗雀，参加展览的代表人员心急如焚。这时一个小徒弟不小心碰掉了一个展台上的酒坛子，只听“哗啦”一声，酒坛破裂，美酒沿着破碎处流了出来，一时间酒香四溢，飘满了整个展馆。代表团的负责人刚要发火，可看到满满围拢过来的人群，他得意地笑了。

接着吩咐伙计们打开一坛酒来，倒在陶瓷碗里，供来往的游客分享。倒出的美酒飘出的香味吸引了更多的人群，他们纷纷过来品尝美酒，赞叹之声不绝于耳。由此，茅台毫无悬念地成为了当年酒类评比的宠儿。而那个默默无闻的酒坛也成了茅台的重要象征，经历过现场的参观者们，每当看到酒坛就想起了美味的茅台酒，于是乎酒坛也随之热了起来。

①

小夫妻与酒瓶

这是一个关于小夫妻间与酒瓶的故事，一个小小的酒瓶见证了彼此之间爱情的真挚和永恒。

话说男孩和女孩终于结婚了，好久宾客们才走。两人在床上聊了好久，熄灯前，男孩一本正经地说：我这里有两瓶酒，一瓶酒我们现在来喝，以庆祝我们的婚姻，一瓶酒放到我们分手的时候喝，以纪念我们的婚姻。女孩子一听有些不快，刚刚结婚就说分手，太不吉利了，但男孩没有解释，她也就没有多问。不过她只看到了一瓶酒，并没有看到第二瓶酒。男孩只是告诉她两瓶酒的瓶子一模一样，今晚过后，明天他就会将它摆在客厅的最显眼处，以提醒彼此珍惜现在的婚姻，珍惜彼此。

一瓶酒就在小两口的互诉衷肠中见了底儿，第二天，正如男孩所说的一个与昨晚一模一样的一瓶酒摆在了客厅的最显眼处。不过女孩看上去特别的眼熟，总感觉这个酒瓶似曾相识。而昨晚的酒瓶自从喝光了之后就再没见过，好像人间蒸发了一般。不过这并不影响两人的恩爱。每天当他们看到这个酒瓶的时候，就会想起可能的分手，于是越发的珍惜当前的拥有，两人之间的情感比结婚前更深厚了。

然而随着时间的推移，男孩的工作越来越忙，经常是十天半个月见不到人。俩人在一起的时间也越来越少，即使见面也说不了几句话，仿佛陌生人一样。女孩怀疑男孩在外面有了女人，于是便专门请了假去跟踪男孩。然而半个月下来，男孩除了生意上的应酬外，几乎很少与别的女孩接触。就是不回家也是在单位里打地铺度过，然而越是这样，女孩越是怀疑男孩有问题，于是每当男孩回家时，她便会借机发脾气，弄得男孩最后连家都不敢回了。

①国酒妙酿琼浆玉液
②宜兴太华镇善卷活动

如此一来，女孩的怀疑心更重了，她甚至大白天跑到男孩的单位去闹。终于男孩忍受不住了，向女孩提出了分手。女孩这时候也忍受了长期的怀疑折磨，想尽快结束这段婚姻生活。在他们分手的那天，两人想起了客厅里的那瓶酒，于是准备在家里吃过最后的晚餐后，明天去办手续。

红红的烛光照在两人的脸上，气氛显得十分的压抑。俩人谁都不想先开口说话，男孩看了看女孩，取出了那瓶已经被尘封的酒，上面的灰尘落了很厚的一层。他一圈圈的启开了上面封着的红绸子，拔掉了瓶塞。给两人分别倒了一杯，然后举杯看着女孩说："我以为这辈子都不可能打开它了，没想到我们最终还是走到了这一步。那么……"男孩哭了。

女孩的心里也不好受，她举起酒杯与男孩碰了一下后就一仰脖喝了下去。奇怪的是，这酒淡得就像白开水一样，丝毫没有前一瓶酒的那种醇香与浓烈。她怀疑地又拿起酒瓶倒了一杯，喝了一口下去，味道还是跟刚才一样，只是比前一杯好像苦了一些，细细品味后，又觉得有些甜。

她疑惑地看了看男孩，希望能从他那里得到解释，男孩没有回答，只是把刚起下来的瓶塞给了女孩。女孩看到瓶塞后，一个大红的喜字映入了眼帘，这不就是新婚之夜他们喝的那瓶酒的瓶塞吗，难道这瓶里不是酒是……女孩的疑问从男孩的脸上得到了答复。

男孩告诉女孩从来没有什么第二瓶酒，所谓的第二瓶酒只是一个善意的谎言。从他们走到一起时开始，他就认定了女孩，无论发生什么事儿他都将跟女孩一起走下去。之所以要把这个瓶子灌上水摆在客厅里，是为了提醒自己要永远珍惜女孩，永远珍惜这个家。同时也提醒自己，婚后的生活就如同这酒瓶里的水一样，最初的浓烈醇香没有了，留下的只是如白开水一样的生活，里面有苦有甜，全在自己品味。

女孩听后，号啕大哭了起来。积压在心里多日的不快一下子全部发泄了出来，这一晚，男孩和女孩谈了好久，第二天，两人都没有去上班，而是去了旅行社。他们决定通过旅行来庆祝彼此的爱情。而那个瓶子仍然被摆放在了客厅的最显眼处，因为它见证着两人的爱情和婚姻。

两只酒瓶的不同遭遇

陶瓷酒瓶葫芦与长脖是一对好兄弟，他们同时被制造出来，又同时被装罐售卖。但是长脖的运气不太好，买它的人是一个酒鬼，在酒被喝完后就被扔在了地上。后来看到一辆马车过来，它就想把马车垫翻，以宣泄自己的怨气，结果被路过的马车碾成碎片，蹦了一地。生气的长脖越想越生气，这时看到一个小孩过来，便上去给小孩的脚划了道口子。小孩流着血跑去向父母告状，生气的父母就把这些碎片扫到一处，倒进了大海，从此长脖永远消失。

而葫芦就幸运多了，它被一个人买走后，便放在了一个柜子里。很长时间都没有人问询，但是它并不生气，而是心平气和地与肚子里的酒和周围的空气交流着。酒在它的肚子里变得越来越香，而它也因为酒变得越来越滋润。不知道过了多长时间，柜子被重新打开，一个人用刷子清理了它身上的尘土，然后用笔小心地编号后，将它放在了一个木头的柜子里，周围是一些陌生的白色东西，软软的，但是很舒服。后来它感觉自己被搬上了一辆车，经过颠簸之后，它被放进了一个更加阴冷的地窖之中。它感觉自己这下完了，不过想到还有酒和周围的箱子陪着自己，心情又开朗了起来。

又不知过了多少个年月，一群考古学家发现了这处地窖，葫芦再次重见天日。因为酒的滋润和良好的心态，它的外形保存完好，受到了文物专家的关注。最后它被摆放在了一个博物馆里，每天接受着来往游客的观赏，心里甭提有多高兴了，也许你不经意地走过一个展柜时，看到一个浑身发亮，充满着润泽光感的酒瓶时，那可能就是它了。

二、与宜兴紫砂陶瓷酒器文化相关的民谣、民谚

民谣、民谚是反映一个地方风土民情的重要方式，很多古老的文化和传承就是通过流传于民间的口头谚语、俗语得以保存下来的。不同时代的酒器，如杯、盏、觥、筹、盅、缸、瓶等，都或多或少的融入到当时的百姓生活之中，成为他们生活起居的重要伙伴。下面我们就通过这些谚语、俗语或歇后语等，了解一下酒器的变化。

谚语俗语

千年老窖万年糟。
戒酒要戒头一盅，戒烟要戒头一口。
茶七饭八酒满盅。
酒喝头杯，茶吃二盏。
卖酒的问提壶的要钱。
饭前三盅酒，饭后一袋烟。
酒逢知己千杯少，能喝多少喝多少，喝不了赶紧跑。
会喝壹桶的喝壹缸，酒厂厂长让你当！
锄禾日当午，汗滴禾下土，连干三杯酒，你说苦不苦？
春眠不觉晓，处处闻啼鸟，举杯问大哥，我该喝多少？
结识新朋友，不忘老朋友。——与新老朋友共干一杯
危难之处显身手，妹妹（兄弟）替哥喝杯酒。
要让客人喝好，自家先要喝倒！
商品经济大流通，开放搞活喝两盅。
酒逢知己千杯少，话不投机大口喝
若要人不知，除非你干杯
天蓝蓝，海蓝蓝，一杯一杯往下传
天上无云地下旱，刚才那杯不能算
百川到东海，何时再干杯，现在不喝酒，将来徒伤悲

1

中华老字号

宜兴金鱼紫砂陶瓷酒瓶烧造技艺·民间文学与诗赋

①宜兴丝弦
②宜兴庙会
③十番锣鼓
④男欢女嬉

宜兴地区民谣　窑场歌谣

唱蜀山

说蜀山，唱蜀山，东坡书院在蜀山，
蜀山顶上祠山败，　三姑娘娘姐妹三，
说蜀山，唱蜀山，制壶匠人出蜀山，
喝汤吃粥黄泥饭，西北风吹进破衣衫，
说蜀山，唱蜀山，匠人做得像泥菩萨，
窑货高过黄龙山。

窑货船

手里忙忙嘴里忙，橹把头干钱也干，
篙子没水钱没钱，窑货船，没个歇脚点，
一天要搁浅，肚皮饿到脊梁骨。

十二月

正月坐过，
二月盘过，
三月呒事做，
四五六月借债过，
七死八活九还魂。
十月忙一忙，
十一月里心发愁，
十二月受冻又挨饿。

泥场

吃的泥灰饭，
干的牛马活，
鸡叫起床干，
太阳落山息。
风吹一半，
雨落全无，
喔哟哟，
叫我怎么过活。

工钱

端阳算算，
八月半看看，
年夜结结账，
剩勿到一半。

做坯

泥料拍拍，
只够嘴里嗒嗒。
泥坯做得光亮，
人和叫花子一样。

买米

背挑八木则，两腿酸煞则，爬到嵩山界，
麻绳绑起则，扁担丢落则，张渚去不成，
遇上丘八则，米么充公则，肚皮饿煞则，
自家吓煞则，老婆急煞则。

（八木则：挑米工具。“则”是借音，意“了”。第四句“丘八则”，即丘八子，谓兵。其余各句的“则”皆句末语气词，也有“了”的意思。）

学艺难

学艺难，学艺难，
好像要上剪刀山。
偷摸偷看暗里做，
东掩西藏躲老板。
深夜挑盏油盏头，
白天担水又砍柴，
鞋底沾回泥一块，
三年五载出师难。

经商谣

一分行情一分货。
一回生，二回熟。
一回上当，两回心亮。
三句话不离本行。
百货中百客，好货迎远客。
出门看天气，买卖看行情。
面带三分笑，生意跑不了。
人无笑脸勿开店。
不怕店门小，就怕货勿好。
生意不成人情在。
不怕不识货，就怕货比货。
中了早客，不中水客。
随行就市，将本求利。
穿靴戴帽，各有所好。
柜台站几年，见人能相面。

上龙窑

上龙窑，上龙窑，
不是腿断就伤腰，
抬不起头，直不起腰，
碰碰窑砖就起泡，
窑内火焰山，
窑外雪花飘，
饥寒炎热都尝到。
一不小心就感冒。
一年到头上龙窑，
人像猢狲难到梢。

宜兴地区生活谣

有志勿在年高
三家人家合只牛，牵来牵去剩个头
千金难买心中愿
只有千里的人情，没有千里的威风
礼多人勿怪
一句话说到人笑，一句话说得人跳
水牛背上拔根毛。（意为微不足道）
穷不贪，富不爱
好歇要做，好吃要饿。
屋有千间，总少一间。
跟好道学好样。
自小看看，到老一半。
贪小利屙大痢。
秧好稻好，娘好妮好。
大家一条心，黄土变成金。
忙忙碌碌，吃鱼吃肉。
小猪吃奶，轧勿上档。
人要面孔树要皮。
邻舍好，赛金宝。
勤俭节约，知足常乐。
无病就是福。
做贼偷菜起，赌钱丁背始。
人勤土变金，人懒地生草。
若要小儿安，常带三分饥和寒。
抽头聚赌，胜如杀人放火。
若要人敬己，必先己敬人。

中华老字号

宜兴金鱼紫砂陶瓷酒瓶烧造技艺·民间文学与诗赋

要知山上路，须问樵柴人。
穷人不生病，就是交好运。
好记心，勿如赖笔头。
一年亏空十年穷，十年亏空一世穷。
早起三日当一工。
二尺二寸手臂，自创自立。
勿要求人落下风。
喊破嗓子，不如做出样子。
话多不灵，食多无味。
身上穿得绸披披，家里没有夜饭米。
打劫一半，火烧全无。
又要马儿跑得快，又要马儿不吃草。
饭后百步，胜开药铺。
越吃越馋，越歇越懒。
硬树自有硬虫钻。
宁在人前全不会，莫在人前会不全。
严是爱，宽是害。
扁担是条龙，一世吃勿穷。
蚂蚁搬空泰山。
樵了一冬柴，煮锅烂巴饭。
（旧社会穷人入不敷出）
鱼有鱼路，虾有虾路。
叫花子上阶沿，得一步进一步。
满饭好吃，满话难讲。
舌头打个滚，叫人不蚀本。
有话不在多说，有理不在声高。
金张渚，银湖父，折只本，上戴埠。
灶窠划划断，水缸挑挑满。

1

歇后语

井罐里放猪心

——尽管（井罐）放心

丁山人卖窑货

——硬碰硬

尿鳖子打酒

——差壶了

长虫爬进酒瓶里

——进退两难

醋坛里打酒

——满不在乎（壶）

醋坛里酿酒

——坛坛酸

打酒只问提壶人

——错不了

喝酒不拿盅子

——胡（壶）来

尿壶里打酒

——不是个家伙

酒杯掉在酒坛里

——罪（醉）上加罪（醉）

酒盅搬家

——离壶了

酒杯里拌黄瓜

——兜不转　（雷同）

酒杯里量米

——小气（器）

酒店里吵架

——胡（壶）闹

酒盅里拌黄瓜

——施展不开　（雷同）

酒杯子里洗澡

——小人

中华老字号

宜兴金鱼紫砂陶瓷酒瓶烧造技艺·民间文学与诗赋

①三跳道情
②故事集
③唱春
④宜兴张渚镇里五村社日活
⑤丁蜀镇老街

三、与宜兴陶瓷酒器文化相关的诗、辞、歌、赋

酒从其诞生的那一刻起就与诗、歌等有着难以割舍的情分，尤其是后来随着中国士大夫阶层的兴起，酒与酒器更成为他们生活中的重要部分，每到聚会、赋诗、填词、唱歌时，均离不开这些酒及酒器。所以这些历朝历代的诗歌，不仅反映了当时的饮酒文化，更反映了当时的酒器文化和酒器的变迁，如中国历史上曾经出现的杯、盏、觥、筹、盅、缸、瓶等，都可以从这些诗、辞、歌、赋中找到。

为此春酒，以介眉寿。
朋酒其飨，曰杀牛羊。
称彼兕觥，万寿无疆。

——《诗经·豳风七月》

操余弧兮反沦降，
援北斗兮酌桂浆。

——屈原《楚辞·东君》

斗酒相娱乐，聊厚不为溥；
驱车策驽马，游戏宛与洛。

——《古诗十九首》

我有一樽酒，欲以赠远人：
愿子留斟酌，叙此平生亲。

——《别诗》

置酒高殿上，亲友从我游。
中厨办丰膳，烹羊宰肥牛。
秦筝何慷慨，齐瑟和且柔。
阳阿奏奇舞，京洛出名讴。
乐饮过三爵，缓带倾庶羞。
主称千年寿，宾奉万年酬。

——曹植《箜篌引》

葡萄美酒夜光杯，欲饮琵琶马上催。
醉卧沙场君莫笑，古来征战几人回。

——王翰《凉州词》

花间一壶酒，独酌无相亲。
举杯邀明月，对影成三人。
月既不解饮，影徒随我身。
暂伴月将影，行乐须及春。
我歌月徘徊，我舞影零乱。
醒时同交欢，醉后各分散。
永结无情游，相期邈云汉。

——李白《月下独酌》

绿蚁新醅酒，红泥小火炉。
晚来天欲雪，能饮一杯无。

——白居易《问刘十九》

将军玉帐貂鼠衣，手持酒杯看云飞。

——刘伯温《北风行》

土是有生之母，陶为人所化生，
陶人与土配成双，天地阴阳酝酿，
水火木金协调，宫商角徵交响，
汇成陶海叹汪洋，真是森罗万象。

——郭沫若《西江月·颂陶》

①荆溪十景——铜峰叠翠
②华溪桥
③丁蜀镇老街

金帆陶瓷

生产性方式保护现状

宜兴金鱼紫砂陶瓷酒瓶

烧造技艺

⑫

1 宜兴金鱼紫砂陶瓷酒瓶烧造技艺现场

中华老字号

宜兴金鱼紫砂陶瓷酒瓶烧造技艺·生产性方式保护现状

一、现代生产工艺及技术创新

“发展是一种继承，唯有继承才能发展。”

振兴陶瓷工业，发展陶瓷生产，让陶瓷实现可持续发展和延续是每个陶瓷人需要坚守的理念和承担的责任。那么如何才能实现陶瓷生产的持续性永久存在呢？市场，也只有市场才有发言权。因为唯有市场始终对陶瓷充满旺盛的需求，那么它就永远不会衰败，而且会历久弥新，得到更大的发展空间和前景，而这一切都需要不断的生产工艺改进和技术革新来实现。

作为陶瓷之都的宜兴，在陶瓷的生产工艺改革和技术革新上一直处于国内的排头兵位置，它在紫砂、日用陶、青瓷的发展和革新中取得了很大的成就，尤其是在紫砂与青瓷的糅合及共同发展中，起到了全国的表率作用，而其中重要的推动和实施者便是金鱼陶瓷及其掌门人谈志坚。

青瓷和紫砂要想发展和延续下去，除了从传统中延续智慧，更重要的还是创新。创新是其发展的源泉，创新是当前历史条件下，二者长久发展和保存的必经之路。只有创新，才能振兴。创新的源泉在哪里？主要就在于传统的青瓷、紫砂制作工艺中，就在于市场的现实需求及未来需求中。联合国教科文组织在《世界文化多样性宣言》中这样宣称：“文化遗产——创作的源泉。每项创作都来源于有关的文化传统，但也在同其他文化传统的交流中得到充分的发展。”这一说法，对于我们的陶瓷业文化遗产的保护与开发有着积极的作用，他告诉我们现实的改革和创新要立足于前人丰富的经验、智慧、灵感和信念基础上，唯有深入挖掘传统的制瓷、制砂工艺，认真研究和实践，才能从中找到创新的灵感和突破口，才能实现生产方式的保护和传承，也才能实现现代生产工艺和技术的改进与创新。

目前陶瓷业的技术创新主要遵循以下几点：

第一，从传统工艺入手，汲取其中的营养和闪光点。传统工艺之所以能够代代传承，长盛不衰，除历史的必然性外，也有着其他生产工艺无法企及的优点和长处，而这正是我们需要认真研究的地方。将其归纳出来，用于现实的生产工艺创新和改进中，就可以起到事半功倍的效果，同时也有助于传统工艺精髓的传承和保护。

第二，借鉴现代工艺的手法和技术，为传统工艺注入现代的元素和特征。传统之所以能够永久传承，关键就在于人们生活的需要和依赖，一旦生活中不再需要这种东西，那么它就会很快消亡。所以要使传统的青瓷、紫砂永久的传承下去，那么就要利用现代的一些先进技术和科技来改造他落

①

②

③

④

⑤

①注浆
②修瓶嘴
③装瓶口
④⑤回浆
⑥绞坯
⑦高位注浆流水线
⑧修坯
⑨烧成
⑩检验

后的生产工艺和环境，使其更加符合现代人的生活理念和审美需求，这也是青瓷、紫砂经千年传承得以历久弥新的关键所在。如现代高温技术、电脑制图技术、现代一体成型工艺、冷成型技术、自动化温控技术、高科技质量检验技术、现代高温传导技术、高科技高温耐火技术、节能环保技术等，与陶瓷生产有着这样或那样的交叉。它们中的部分已经被一些陶瓷生产企业所引用和借鉴，成为生产中改造窑炉、控制炉温、检测成品的重要组成部分，提高着青瓷、紫砂的生产水平，使陶瓷成批量生产成为可能。

第三，就地取材（找材），就地变材（配比），提高生产的灵活性和自由度。我们知道陶土资源的发现是一个漫长的历史过程，是一个不断的实验、失败、再实验、再失败直至成功的过程，所以我们现代的生产也不能太过拘泥于古老的经验和材料，而应该放宽思维，从更广阔的角度来寻找解决问题的答案。尤其是目前现有陶土资源紧张，紫砂泥资源更是难得的基础上，努力寻找其替代品和别的实现方法，力求在保证传统的基础上，使其更加体现现代生活对于材质环保、绿色的诉求。而这也是我们对于传统制作技艺精髓的真正继承。

第四，工艺革新，让紫砂及青瓷制品更具有时代的色彩和特色。所有工艺，只有在为时代所需求时，他才能真正得到传承，否则只能慢慢地走向消亡，紫砂、青瓷的生产也是如此。就当代宜兴青瓷的创新而言，新青瓷技艺以浓缩着技艺的秘密、历史的信息、独特的思想而闻名。它之所以能够不断地得到社会的青睐与喜爱，就在于当代的青瓷作品，反映出了人们在青瓷这种材料上倾注的复杂细致劳动，及赋予的深厚中国文化内涵与中国审美情趣，它们在继承传统工艺的基础上融入了现代的生产理念和造型艺术，是其在体现古典和传统的同时，反映了时代的诉求和喜好，从而成为青瓷技艺发展的忠实而又独特的物证，成为时代的宠儿。

⑥

⑦

⑧

⑨

⑩

中华老字号

宜兴金鱼紫砂陶瓷酒瓶烧造技艺·生产性方式保护现状

第五，现代造型理念和色彩科学引入紫砂及青瓷的生产实践中，使其更具有时代的特色和表征。古朴端庄的造型为人民所喜爱，但接受者十分有限，唯有充满着时代气息，体现着现代文明与时尚的东西，才能最终成为市场的最爱。所以，进行生产工艺改进与创新时，需紧密结合时代和需求，要知道市场才是我们改革成功与否的最终检验者，如果市场给出了否决票，那么再精致的创新、再深入的改革也是没有用的，只能是将传统工艺带入死胡同，而无法让其发挥功用。所以要推动技术的改革和创新，让传统工艺不断展现出新的华彩，并永远地传承下去，那么引入时代因素，注入现代理念，向市场要发展，将是我们重要的出路之一。

第六，生产工艺的改进与革新要深入到整个生产环节中去，使其成为一个系统化的工程。也就是我们要深入进整个陶瓷产业现代化的生产过程中去，从产业的装备、营销、展示、品牌、物流、环保、设计、辅料等诸多配套上着手进行改进和提升，否则所有的一切都将成为空谈。金鱼陶瓷这几年的飞速发展和提升，就是得益于这种系统化的改进和发展，才使它成为行业的翘楚，紫砂陶瓷酒瓶界的NO.1。而近几年的其他传统手工艺的发展，也佐证了这一观点，如剪纸、木版画、年画、景泰蓝等。

以上仅仅是列举了现代生产工艺和技术创新中的一些典型方式和方法，我们相信在现实的生产和生活中还有着更好更多的方法和手段可以为传统手工技艺的传承提供帮助和助力，只是由于信息或创新者本身商业机密的考量，未能对外公布。不过，看到金鱼陶瓷今天的成就以及它对宜兴青瓷及紫砂的带动性改革示范作用，我们有理由相信在不远的将来，宜兴青瓷及紫砂一定会从流传了几千年的模式中逐渐蜕变，产生出一种既结合着传统又融合着现代、既结合着中国又融合着西方的新的青瓷、紫砂制造工艺，而且以其旺盛的活力得到更好的传承与发展。

二、从生产性方式保护层面看宜兴金鱼紫砂陶瓷酒瓶烧造技艺的独特性

（一）技艺的创新特色

“只有站在前人的肩上，才能看到未来的发展之路。”

在探讨了现代紫砂及青瓷生产工艺和技术的创新之后，我们再来具体看看宜兴金鱼紫砂陶瓷酒瓶烧造技艺在创新中所体现的特色和不同之处，以及它由亏损走向盈利，由当年名不见经传而成为国内数一数二的紫砂陶瓷酒瓶NO.1的关键所在。

第一，改造原有生产窑炉，有效控制了炉温，降低了生产的消耗，提高了成品率和成品的质量，使紫砂陶瓷酒瓶实现了批量化生产。工厂原有的德式窑成品率低，耗能大，温度无法精确掌控，对于生产紫砂陶瓷酒

①球磨机
②搅拌石膏

瓶来说，是一大问题，而传统的土窑虽然适合紫砂的烧制，但对于烧制紫砂陶瓷酒瓶却无能为力，为此在金鱼陶瓷掌门人谈志坚的带领下，对原有的窑炉进行了改进，在融合传统窑炉特色的基础上，采用了先进的高温节能技术、电脑自动检测技术等，扩大了原有的窑炉规模，减小了能耗，降低了紫砂陶瓷酒瓶的废品率，提升了产品的质量，并使得批量化生产紫砂陶瓷酒瓶成为可能。

第二，改进了制瓶工具，尤其是制瓶模具，使其更加耐用，更加精细，有利于控制酒瓶的大小和形制，同时对于控制酒瓶的最终容积和成品效果也提供了保证。这种改进适应了酒瓶规模化、标准化、批量化生产的要求，使其在短时间里生产出批量合格的产品成为可能，为金鱼陶瓷赢得市场、稳定顾客提供了有力的保障。

第三，紫砂陶瓷酒瓶工艺的成型及改进。我们知道紫砂具有天然的气孔，砂粒与砂粒之间具有一定的间隙，这对于泡茶来说是一定的好事，可以提高茶香，保持茶的新鲜。但对于做酒瓶来说，却始终是一个致命的问题。因为它会增加酒的挥发和渗漏风险，不宜于酒的长久保存。因而长久以来，虽然有人想到过使用它来做酒瓶，但囿于这一技术难题始终未能如愿。金鱼陶瓷则在谈志坚的领导下攻克了这一难题，他将传统的瓶内施釉技术与紫砂制作工艺结合，从而生产出了高质量的紫砂陶瓷酒瓶，从而填补了国内这一块的空白，成为紫砂陶瓷酒瓶界的开创者和NO.1。在开发此项技术时，除了两种传统工艺的融合，它还通过利用现代技术改造了原有的生产窑炉，使其温度处于可控的范围内，这为紫砂烧制与釉的烧制不同温度提供了可能，从而最终实现了紫砂陶瓷酒瓶的生产。

第四，造型工艺的突破。金鱼陶瓷的紫砂陶瓷酒瓶在设计酒瓶时，打破了传统的酒瓶形制限制，而更多地考虑客户的需求和顾客的品位，将传统美学和实用主义相互结

合，从而设计出了深受顾客欢迎，同时又符合客户要求和产品特色的酒瓶来，使其无论在形制还是文化上都实现了完美的效果，为其赢得客户，打开销路提供了助力。同时也为传统紫砂制作工艺及瓶内施釉工艺的传承提供了可能。

第五，外部装饰融入现代造型手法和色彩理念，运用电脑制图一次成型，并通过电脑控制制作模具，既使产品拥有了时尚美观的外形，又实现了批量化的标准化生产，在承袭传统模具制作工艺的基础上，融入了现代的质量管控体系，提高了产品的质量和生产效率。

第六，紫砂陶瓷酒瓶的制作承袭传统的制作要求，兼顾形、气、神，注重泥料的选取和不同原料的配比，同时对生产过程中的工艺进行严格的管控和磨砺，从而最终实现了既保持传统手工技艺的特色，同时又不失现代批量化生产的需求特征，完美地达到了预期的效果和目的。开创了紫砂陶瓷酒瓶的先河，创造了新的历史和工艺。

这就是宜兴金鱼紫砂陶瓷酒瓶制器人苦苦耕耘乃至凝聚毕生心血的创新过程。这是一种不怕困难，勇往直前的开拓精神，也是一种继承传统，深入挖掘，推陈出新的创举。从宏观的角度来看，它暗含了中国非物质文化遗产保护工程自启动以来的种种尝试，也体现了非物质文化遗产保护的重要积极意义。

（二）与区域内相似产品的对比

“所谓的不同，其实是源于用心的结果。”

金鱼紫砂陶瓷酒瓶的存在并非一个孤立的现象，同其他的传统手工技艺产品一样，它也有很多同类的产品存在。不过鉴于商业竞争的存在，不同的产品又有着各自独特的配方和制作工艺，最终的产品也会呈现出不同的特性和功用。

我们就以金鱼紫砂陶瓷酒瓶为例，来对比它与区域内其他相似产品的不同：

1．制作工艺更加复杂精细。与传统的陶瓷酒瓶相比，紫砂陶瓷酒瓶的生产无论是在内部施釉还是烧制成型中，都需要投入更多的人力和物力，所使用的窑炉也有别于其他的窑炉，而是经过特殊的改装和处理之后的。

2．用料上更加讲究和科学。为了保障施釉后紫砂不会出现爆裂的问题，在紫砂泥的原料配比上，紫砂陶瓷酒瓶要有别于其他同类紫砂产品，除选料时更加苛刻严格外，在不同原料间的配比上也有着严格的规定和比例，一分一毫都不可疏忽。

3．造型上更加大胆和创新。金鱼紫砂陶瓷酒瓶打破了原有的酒瓶造型和设计理念，启用全新的电脑一次成型和建模技术，使得成品的形制更加可控，更加具有操作的自由度。在具体的造型中，除吸取传统的造型特点之外，还加入了客户的产品诉求和理念，让酒瓶更加契合客户的产品，符合其产品的定位。从而开创了酒瓶定制和个性化生产的路子。

4．紫砂陶瓷酒瓶的出现，既保持了紫砂古朴高雅充满着古典主义色彩的外观特色，同时又利用内部施釉，使其可以实现其他紫砂酒具所无法实现的防渗漏问题。从而大大提升了紫砂酒瓶的实用功能，满足了市场对于紫砂酒瓶的需求。同时该产品还保留了紫砂器皿良好的呼吸性能，使得酒瓶内的酒可以实现再次发酵，从而更加醇美可口。

5．不同于其他产品的分阶段监控和生产方式。金鱼紫砂陶瓷酒瓶从产品设计、制模成型到拉坯、制作、烧制直至后续的营销、运输、包装、宣传、回访，进行全程的跟踪和监督，以实现产品的最佳使用和呈现效果。这样既保障了客户的利益，适应了现代市场的需求，同时又可以及时发现客户的诉求、了解产品的问题和遗漏，从而为产品的改进与更新提供了方便。

鉴于以上几点，金鱼紫砂陶瓷酒瓶得以屹立于众多酒瓶生产厂家之中，而异军突起，独占鳌头。我们有理由相信，金鱼草陶的这种创新方式和理念对于我们传统的手工技艺的传承和发展将起到标杆式的作用，成为非物质文化遗产保护的一个活的案例，引导和促进我们对于传统的继承和发扬。

三、宜兴金鱼紫砂陶瓷酒瓶烧造技艺的传播与文化思考

"其开创性的意义远大于继承和发扬，但却为继承和发扬提供了借鉴和参考。"

宜兴金鱼紫砂陶瓷酒瓶烧造技艺是我国传统紫砂制作技艺与陶瓷酒瓶制作技艺在新时代的全新融合和展示，也是对于传统工艺的一种创新与发展。这种创新式的融合，对于我国今后此类产品及同类技艺的传承与发展提供了一个范例和方向，也为我们进行非物质文化遗产的研究和保护提供了思考和调研的角度。

1．历史及文化价值

陶瓷是我国伟大的发明，早在新石器时代时期，人们就已经开始了简单的陶器制作，发展至今已衍生出很多独特的品种和种类，并诞生了一批有着独特文化色彩和个性魅力的制作技艺与手法。宜兴金鱼紫砂陶瓷酒瓶就是在这样的一个基础上产生并发展起来的。它不是某个独立技术的发展与创新，而是立足于整个紫砂制作和青瓷制作基础上的一个融合和创新。在其改革和发展的过程中，他撇开了一般的门户之见，将不同的传统制作工艺和手法融会在一起，取其长处，来开放新的产品和工艺。在融会古老的制作技艺的同时，它还广泛借鉴了其他行业的制作工艺和手法，并积极吸纳最新的科技成果和理念，将其运用到现实的生产和创作中，从而缔造了像紫砂陶瓷酒瓶这样跨时代的新品，填补了我国在这一领域的空白，跻身世界前列，我们古老的陶瓷文化再次走向世界，引领世界潮流提供了实践的意义。

其造型上也广泛吸纳中国传统的绘画、雕刻、书法及诗歌艺术，并融入现代的几何造型理念，让原有的酒瓶形制在保持传统的基础上，展现出了新的风采和魅力。在体现古典的文化和传承的基础上，具有了时代的特征和文化标榜，从而更加凸显其作为这一时代产品的特色和表征。

2．学术及科学价值

陶瓷自产生以来，就处于不断的改进和发展之中，我们现在所看到的很多传统的制瓷工艺就是经过千百年来的不断改进和创新，历经大浪淘沙般的遴选而保留下来的。所以我们研究传统的陶瓷制作工艺就要深入到不同的时代中去，通过分析不同的时代特色和市场需求，来寻找技术改进的动力和源泉，从而找出技术改进发展的趋势和方向，为我们现在传统技艺保护和继承提供依据和借鉴。

金鱼紫砂陶瓷酒瓶烧造技艺对于传统紫砂制作技艺和传统酒瓶制作工艺的继承和改进给我们研究传统的工艺提供了一个方向和借鉴，也从学术和科研角度进行此类非物质文化遗产的保护和发扬提供了思路。通过对金鱼紫砂陶瓷酒瓶制作工艺及市场影响的研究，我们得出对于此类手工艺来说，最好的研究方式就是深入到当时的社会环境中去，通过对当时科技水平和先进技艺的研究以及市场需求的愿望，总结出技术之所以得到继承和改进的原因，从而为今后同类手工技艺的传承和发展提供一个方向性的指导和方式上的借鉴。金鱼紫砂陶瓷酒瓶的开创性意义便在于此，它不仅给我们的非物质文化遗产保护提供了一个思路，而且为今后的发展和继承提供了一个可资借鉴的案例。从这个意义上来说，它是值得我们肯定和推荐的。对于宜兴金鱼紫砂陶瓷酒瓶烧造技艺进行深入地考察研究，既是对传统陶瓷技艺的探究，也是对宜兴陶瓷技艺传承现状的考察，更是对宜兴陶瓷技艺发展机遇的认识，无疑具有重要的学术价值和实践意义。

3．社会及经济价值

从20世纪90年代初开始，金鱼紫砂陶瓷酒瓶开始在国内外影响日隆，其掌门人谈志坚已成为一个重要的名牌表征，赢得整个市场的认可和客户的肯定，而由其烧制进行的窑炉改造和技术革新对于市场同类产品也起到了积极的推进作用。尤其是其窑炉改造成功经验的推行，为同类行业的生产节省了能源，提高了成品率和产品质量，为传统技艺在新时代的发展提供了助力。

由金鱼陶瓷开创的系列紫砂陶瓷酒瓶弥补了国内在这一方面的不足，同时为其他同类产品的改革和创新提供了思路和借鉴，引起了新一轮陶瓷酒瓶的制作和创新热潮。同时也奠定了金鱼陶瓷在业界的领导地位，为其获得了很好的社会效益和经济效益，很多知名的厂家，如茅台、五粮液、口子窖等都成为其忠实的客户，从而为其进一步开拓市场提供了方便和助力。

非物质文化遗产档案

中华老字号·宜兴金鱼紫砂陶瓷酒瓶烧造技艺

China Time-honored Brand · Baking Crafts of Yixing Goldfish Purple Ceramic Wine Bottle

孙冬宁／著

Composer Sun Dongning

文化藝術出版社

Culture and Art Publishing House

图书在版编目(CIP)数据

宜兴金鱼紫砂陶瓷酒瓶烧造技艺 / 孙冬宁著. －北京：

文化艺术出版社，2011.12

（非物质文化遗产档案. 中华老字号）

ISBN 978-7-5039-5287-6

Ⅰ.①宜… Ⅱ.①孙… Ⅲ.①紫砂陶－酒瓶－

工艺美术－宜兴市 Ⅳ.①J527

中国版本图书馆CIP数据核字(2011)第258802号

非物质文化遗产档案：中华老字号

——宜兴金鱼紫砂陶瓷酒瓶烧造技艺

著　　者：孙冬宁

责任编辑：蔡宛若

装帧设计：藝術團隊

孙冬宁、刘磊、王颖

承　　制：山东非物质文化遗产研究中心"老字号"设计艺术研究所

出版发行：文化艺术出版社

地　　址：北京市东城区东四八条52号　100007

网　　址：www.whyscbs.com

电子邮箱：whysbooks@263.net

电　　话：(010)84057666(总编室)　84057667(办公室)

(010)84057691－84057699(发行部)

传　　真：(010)84057660(总编室)　84057670(办公室)

(010)84057690(发行部)

经　　销：新华书店

印　　刷：北京方嘉彩色印刷有限责任公司印刷

版　　次：2012年3月第1版

印　　次：2012年3月第1次印刷

开　　本：965×635毫米　1/16

印　　张：16.5

字　　数：200千字

书　　号：ISBN 978-7-5039-5287-6

定　　价：458.00元

版权所有，侵权必究。印装错误，随时调换。

非物质文化遗产档案

中华老字号 · 宜兴金鱼紫砂陶瓷酒瓶烧造技艺

The Intangible Cultural Heritage File

China Time-honored Brand · Yixing Baking Crafts of Yixing Goldfish Purple Ceramic Wine Bottle

山東非物質文化遺産研究中心
Shandong Intangible Cultural Heritage Research Center
老字号文化遗产研究专家
http://www.sdich.com

非物质文化遗产档案

中华老字号·传统技艺

The Intangible Cultural Heritage File

China Time-honored Brand · Traditional Techniques